EXPLORING THE JEMEZ COUNTRY

Second Edition

ROLAND A. PETTITT

Revisions and maps by Dorothy Hoard

D1602422

Los Alamos Historical Society
Los Alamos, New Mexico
1990

Copyright © 1990 by Los Alamos Historical Society
Second Printing 1994

Photographs by Roland A. Pettitt
Additional photographs by John V. Young
Maps by Dorothy Hoard
Design by Gloria Sharp

Technical assistance by
Carol Banks of the Ad Makers
Michael Greenbank of Photos by Michael
Carolyn Wright of The Photography Studio

Library of Congress Cataloging-in-Publication Data

Pettitt, Roland A.
    Exploring the Jemez country / Roland A. Pettitt.—2nd ed. /
revisions and maps by Dorothy Hoard.
        p.   cm.
    ISBN 0-941232-10-7
    1. Jemez Mountains Region (N.M.)—Description and travel—Guide-
books.   2. Automobile travel—New Mexico—Jemez Mountains Region—
Guide-books.   I. Hoard, Dorothy.   II. Title.
F802.S3P48   1990
917.89'57—dc20   90-33924
                                                                         CIP

First edition of *Exploring the Jemez Country*
published by Pajarito Publications, Los Alamos, NM,
and copyright © 1975 by Roland A. Pettitt

Printed in the United States of America

CONTENTS

MAPS

FROM THE PETTITT FAMILY

The trauma of Roland's years of disability has left a lasting impression on our family: enjoy creation and nature each day, there are no guarantees for a tomorrow.

Before being stricken with the pain and complications of his last illness, Roland was actively researching and documenting material for the expansion and revision of *Exploring the Jemez Country*. Although he personally could not reach that goal, a generous and trusted friend has fulfilled that dream for us.

Our gratitude to Dorothy Hoard is beyond measure. Without hesitating a moment, she agreed to revise the book. It meant many hours of hiking, driving, drawing, and writing. Her empathy toward our loss and her gentle skills with pen and words are a blessing to our family. We are very pleased with this tribute to Roland's memory.

In deep appreciation,
Mary (Pettitt) Venable
and children
Jean Pettitt Paff
Susan Pettitt Rome
Jeffrey Pettitt
1989

FOREWORD

When Roland Pettitt died in 1987, an entire community was saddened by the loss. Everyone who met Roland soon realized that he was extraordinary—a man with a broad range of interests who radiated a love for life and people. He cared deeply for the outdoors, especially *his* outdoors in north central New Mexico. It took only a few words about his beloved Jemez before his eyes sparkled and the conversation became filled with recollections, reminiscences, and anticipation of undiscovered treasures. Even when he was paralyzed during his final illness, his heart remained in the mountains. Attempts to revisit favored places in the Jemez made him and his family ardent advocates of access for the handicapped to forest facilities. Several improvements and modifications around the Redondo area are due directly to their efforts.

Exploring the Jemez Country first came out in 1975. In 1989 it is still fresh and relevant and bursting with joy. It has been a delight to update the little book. Not the least of pleasures has been working with people who loved Roland, or his book, or the Jemez Mountains. One can well envy my bouncing over the back

roads with Ken Kutac in his big red truck, or
gliding in style with Doug Venable in his ele-
gant 4 x 4, always with Mary Pettitt as our
gracious hostess. I cajoled son Robin into help-
ing me "check it out" one more time; poured
over maps with cartographer Andi Kron; spent
a fascinating afternoon with Bob Crostic of the
U.S. Forest Service's Jemez District, who later
kindly reviewed the manuscript; iterated the
geological text revisions with a patient Fraser
Goff; expressed profound thanks to Ken Kutac
for reviewing the maps and was charmed by his
interest in ladybugs; admired John Young's new
photos for the book; and cringed when my edi-
tor, Donald Hoard—whose fee is apple pie—
grumbled, "This is a two-pie chapter."

I treasure my association with the Los
Alamos Historical Society. Lore Watt and her
Publications Committee—Kitty Fluharty, Betty
Leffler, and Janice Baker—read, typed, edited,
formatted, clarified, evaluated, and saw the
book through to the end. We thank Evelyn Vigil
for permission to reprint parts of articles by
Roland that first appeared in the *Los Alamos
Monitor.*

Through it all, one fact was obvious: we—and
hundreds more—share the love of our mountains that Roland expressed so eloquently in
Exploring the Jemez Country.

Dorothy Hoard
1989

CAUTIONS

1. Some of the roads described in this book require a 4-wheel drive or high-clearance vehicle. These roads are so indicated on the maps.

2. Forest Service gates marked on the maps may be locked from time to time. Call the local ranger station for current information.

3. Approaching wildlife too closely may be hazardous to your health! Rodents may have fleas that carry plague. Ticks may be infected with Rocky Mountain spotted fever.

4. Carry drinking water with you. Stream water in the Jemez country is unsafe to drink.

5. Watch out for lightning and flash floods in the summer. Guard against hypothermia in the winter.

Information:
　　Jemez District, U.S. Forest Service
　　P.O. Box 98, Jemez Springs, NM 87025
　　(505) 829-3535

　　Bandelier National Monument
　　Los Alamos, NM 87544
　　(505) 672-3861

JEMEZ COUNTRY

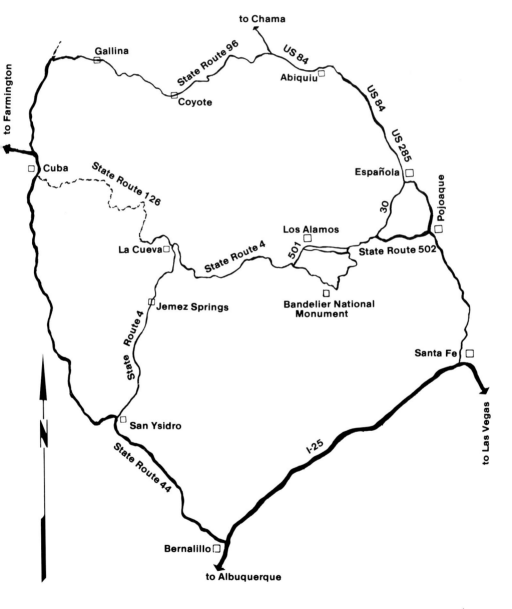

Introduction

When an out-of-stater thinks of New Mexico, visions of desert cactus and sun-bleached bones flash through the mind. Some of New Mexico is like that, but not all. Not by a long, long shot.

Along its northern border, New Mexico wears a crown of green forest sliding down over its forehead like a slightly awry halo. Hidden away within this greenery are deep canyons, sparkling mountain streams, and alpine meadows covered with enough wildflowers to weave cloaks for all the ancient Indian gods that live among the surrounding peaks.

First-time tourists are stirred to exclaim in delight, "But they never told me New Mexico was like this!" That's true; no one ever seems to tell about northern New Mexico as it really is—and that's part of the reason for this book.

Very few people know, for instance, that this part of the Southwest has a distinct rainy season in July and August and that when other areas are turning brown from late summer drought New Mexico is in the height of its lushness.

Then comes the beautiful Indian summer weather—truly *el buen tiempo*. There are days upon days of endless blue skies and warm sunshine as the sun retreats southward and the nights grow colder. Autumn ends in a glorious burst of color when the aspens contrast their gold with the dark green of the pine woods. New Mexican wildflowers, sensing the oncoming winter, finish the season in a special cascade of brilliance.

Crown Jewel

The Jemez Mountain Range is one of the brightest gems in this crown of green that New Mexico wears. Set almost squarely in the center

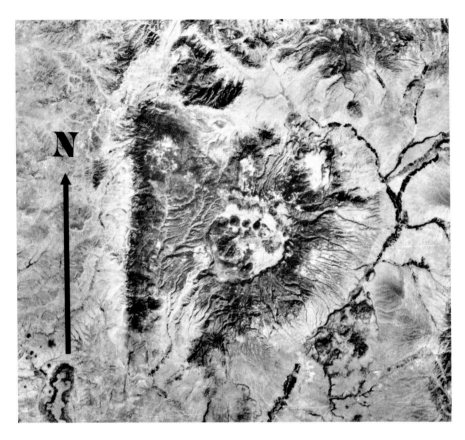

of the state, the Jemez country glows with a glory all its own.

The region is saturated with sculptured reminders of its unique geologic past. The mysticism of its prehistoric people can still be plainly felt. Yet, after a visit to Los Alamos, where the technology of the 21st century is now being initiated, there is the feeling that the mystique of modern science is already blending in with the cultures that have gone before. It's as if the past and the future are all rolled up into the present moment of being—ready to be a source of enjoyment and wonder for those who pause along these mountain pathways.

The Nacimiento Mountains lie just to the west of the Jemez Range. Although epochs

The Jemez Mountains are a dominant feature of north central New Mexico. This Earth Resources Technology Satellite (ERTS) photo, taken on September 2, 1973, from an altitude of 100 miles, shows the circular Valles caldera at the center of the range. The Nacimiento Uplift is the straight, north-south trending scarp to the west (left) of the caldera. The Rio Grande appears as a dark line to the east (right) of the caldera.

3

apart geologically, they are so close together physically that it's almost impossible to tell where one ends and the other begins. Usually, the two are lumped together when people speak of the Jemez country.

The Grand Tour

Fortunately, it's possible to explore nearly all of this area. A network of good highways, forest roads, and hiking trails exists, and most of it is open to public use as either National Forest or National Park Service land.

All-weather highways circle the perimeter of the entire region, making access to the different sections quite easy. State Route 44 from Bernalillo to Bloomfield and U.S. Highway 84 from Santa Fe to Chama mark the western and eastern boundaries respectively, while State Route 96 between Abiquiu Dam and Cuba completes the northern boundary. Another paved road, State Route 4—accessed by way of State Route 502 from Pojoaque—cuts past Bandelier National Monument through the middle of the Jemez, then swings south down the Cañon de San Diego to San Ysidro. An additional road, State Route 126, unpaved for most of its length, leaves State Route 4 at La Cueva and crosses the Nacimiento Mountains to Cuba on the west side.

As an introduction to this land, a "Grand Tour" of the Jemez can be made in about two days. Admittedly, it requires staying on the main roads and doing lots of driving, and such a pace leaves little time for hiking and exploring. However, this trip gives a taste of the different areas. Then, from the main network of roads, future leisurely weekend trips can be taken to fully savor the separate little corners of this oasis in the Land of Enchantment.

4

The different portions of this book are mostly the results of such weekend trips—often impromptu outings when, with family or friends, we piled our camping gear into the car and took off without much planning except for a desire to explore another canyon or mesa. Many of these accounts of our trips have appeared as special features in the *Los Alamos Monitor.*

Perhaps the real attraction of the Jemez is that, as busy as the main roads are, it's possible to get off by yourself. There are canyons for camping where you won't see another person for two days—and back-packing trails where you can be alone for a week.

So, let's get started exploring!

Indian ruins, the remains of ancient dwellings, are scattered the length and breadth of the Jemez Mountains. We and the Santa Fe National Forest are custodians and protectors of this vast cultural heritage.

5

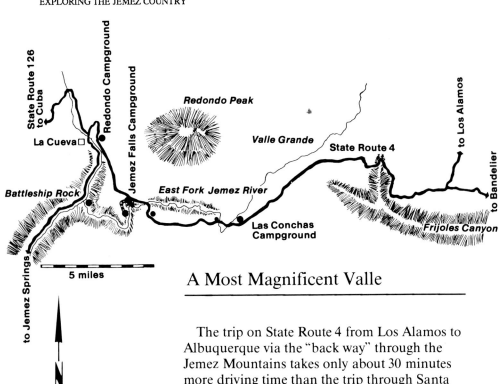

A Most Magnificent Valle

The trip on State Route 4 from Los Alamos to Albuquerque via the "back way" through the Jemez Mountains takes only about 30 minutes more driving time than the trip through Santa Fe. It's not quite 60 miles by road to Zia Pueblo, but within that distance the total essence of New Mexico is captured. From the modern laboratories of Los Alamos to the prehistoric pueblos along the lower Jemez River, the road stretches through four climate zones, encompassing nearly 5,000 years of human endeavor and two billion years of geologic history.

Not a bad bargain for an extra 30 minutes— especially when some of the most spectacular scenery in the Southwest is included along the way.

A day or two spent exploring this wonderland route instills an insight into the full significance of the natural and human history that has occurred here. The area just between Los Alamos and the road junction at La Cueva really deserves a complete day of unhurried sightseeing. A picnic at one of the pretty forest campsites and a few short hikes will uncover perspectives that are otherwise overlooked.

6

Westward from Los Alamos

Approximately four miles beyond the junction of State Route 4 and State Route 501, the highway skirts the northern edge of Frijoles Canyon. The creek on the canyon floor is 1,200 feet below the road. The fact that all of this depth has been cut within volcanic tuff rock gives an indication of the tremendous quantities of ash that spewed out of the Jemez Volcano. Across the canyon lies Obsidian Ridge, the reputed spot from which Indians in the upper Rio Grande Valley obtained obsidian to make their finest arrowheads. Obsidian from this ridge found its way through trading as far as Wyoming and the Great Plains. At night, the lights of Albuquerque can be seen, 50 miles away.

A few miles farther along, up over the rim of the Sierra de los Valles, is the Valle Grande. This valley forms but a small part of the Valles caldera, a collapsed volcano. The rocks, hot springs, and other geologic features of the

Here lies a most magnificent valle. Grassy meadows and meandering streams of the Valle Grande cover the floor of the Valles caldera. The bald slope of Pajarito Mountain lies on the rim of the ancient caldera.

7

The Jemez River plunges 70 feet into a deep gorge near Jemez Falls Campground. An overlook area provides a fine view of the falls.

Jemez Mountains and Valles caldera have been studied extensively for geothermal energy projects. It was once thought that a tremendous mountain 27,000 feet high existed here, but scientists now believe that the landscape was probably similar to the surrounding hills and ridges. There is no reason to believe that the maximum elevation ever exceeded 12,000 feet, which is only about 800 feet higher than Redondo Peak in the center of the caldera.

An Explosive Million Years

To understand the formation of the caldera, go back about 1.1 million years. This area was probably a jumble of broad mountains. Beneath them, a chamber filled with vapor-rich magma exploded. The eruption caused immediate collapse of the roof rocks above the chamber. Nearly 75 cubic miles of glowing ash poured forth. The ash cooled and consolidated into volcanic tuff formations that now cap the plateaus to the south and west. During the eruptions, subsidence formed a caldera 12 miles across and 1,000 feet deep.

During the caldera's first 100,000 years, degassed magma pushing toward the surface lifted Redondo Peak in the center of the depression. Surrounding Redondo Peak, but within the caldera, is a ring of volcanic domes ranging in age from about one million years to 130,000 years. There are also four other valles within the caldera—Valle de los Posos, Toledo, San Antonio, and Jaramillo—but none can match the magnificent Valle Grande in size and beauty.

The great basin filled with water to become a lake, with peaks sticking up as islands. Then about 500,000 years ago San Antonio Creek and the East Fork of the Jemez River cut through the caldera rim and released the impounded waters. Rapid draining of the lake caused a breach in the caldera wall several miles wide.

More volcanic episodes followed, filling canyons and the breached area with ash and lava.
These events left a very complex geologic history for scientists to unravel.

Nearly all of the caldera is now private land,
within the boundaries of the Baca Location
No. 1—so named because of its first ownership.
In 1860, both the town of Las Vegas and the
heirs of Luis Cabeza de Baca possessed valid
claims to 500,000 acres of land where the town
is located. The U.S. Congress, to settle the dis-
puted claims, offered the Baca family five
100,000-acre parcels of unclaimed land of their
own choosing in exchange for relinquishing
their Las Vegas claim. The family accepted and
took as their first choice the 100,000 acres in the
center of the Valles caldera.

Those beautiful outcrops of lichen-covered
rocks on the north side of the road near Las
Conchas Campground are some of the original
wall material of the volcano—formed long
before the final eruptions. At Las Conchas, on
the far side of the creek, a small natural stone
arch has been formed, just the right size for
children to crawl through.

The last volcanism to take place in the Jemez
area originated in the crater now called El
Cajete (Spanish for "flat bowl") on the southern
slope of Redondo Peak. From this spot came
the distinctive "popcorn" pumice beds that are
seen in the road cuts past Las Conchas. Also
from this center emerged the rock with the
poetic name—the Banco Bonito flow. Expo-
sures of this glassy black- and brown-streaked
obsidian are seen along the highway near the
entrance to the Jemez Falls Campground.

**Popcorn pumice from
El Cajete, last of the
volcanic lava flows
from the Valles caldera,
is exposed at road cuts
along State Route 4.**

A Road for All Seasons

Beyond the Valle Grande, State Route 4
winds through the forest past three popular
campgrounds. Las Conchas is first, beside the
Jemez River. Jemez Falls Campground, about

9

six miles farther west, lies a mile south of State Route 4 at the end of a dirt road. Redondo Campground is a jewel tucked among the cinnamon-colored pines. Any one, or all, invite a stop to savor the fragrance and charm of the mountains. Come on a brilliant October day when the aspens shimmer against an impossibly blue sky. On any sunny winter weekend, the highway is lined with vehicles tilted against the snowbanks, while on hidden trails and logging roads, cross-country skiers shed the stress and cares of modern life. Even in spring, when the wind tosses dark spruce boughs and white aspen branches reach toward a leaden sky, while rivulets from old snow fields rush beside the road, it is impossible to resist the magic of the mountains.

Botany at its Best

The forest along State Route 4 is mostly ponderosa pine. Even where the spruce, fir, and aspen predominate, there is still an occasional ponderosa. There are two places, however, where the ponderosas disappear completely— the spruce and fir reign supreme for a short distance where the road breaks over the rim of the Valles caldera and again where the road climbs slightly before dropping into the drainage valley of the East Fork of the Jemez River.

About four miles beyond Las Conchas, one mile before the Jemez Falls turnoff, is East Fork Trailhead, a pretty little rest area. Forest Trail 137 crosses State Route 4 here; leading east or south, it invites hikers and cross-country skiers to experience the full flavor of the caldera forests.

Heading off to the east directly from the trailhead, Trail 137 crosses the mesa for a mile or so, then divides. The north branch soon divides again, with each branch descending to the East Fork of the Jemez River. The west-most (lefthand) branch is the more gentle. Each path

crosses the river on a sturdy—and slightly bouncy—footbridge. The bridges allow a nice loop walk of a quarter mile along the river bank. Back at the top of the mesa, the south branch of Trail 137 wanders east through the ponderosa woods, passing through several aspen groves before dropping down to the river. Then it is about two miles—and seven boulder-hopping creek-crossings—through the box of the river to State Route 4 just around the bend from Las Conchas Campground. The total distance from trailhead to trailhead is five miles.

Across State Route 4 from the East Fork Trailhead, Trail 137 descends south through gently rolling forest groves to Jemez Falls Campground and Jemez Falls. It continues high above the river along the canyon wall all the way down to Battleship Rock, passing a fine hot springs on the way. Total distance, one way, is about five miles.

Across the highway from Redondo Campground is a Forest Service gem: the Jemez Canyon Overlook Trail. Fairly level, surfaced with asphaltic concrete and easily traveled by older folks, the trail features wayside signs at points of botanical interest. And not just run-of-the-mill botany either, but uniquely different bits of forest lore. There are benches for resting and contemplating these varieties of nature's handiwork. (Roland's ashes are scattered here.)

Along the trail at the canyon rim, a cleared spot affords an impressive overview of Jemez Canyon (called Cañon de San Diego on the maps). From this viewpoint, one can see Battleship Rock as well as State Route 4 winding toward Jemez Springs. It's like looking into a trench in time, because down there lie some of the Jemez country's oldest happenings.

Cañon de San Diego cuts south through the mesas. The prow of Battleship Rock appears in the middle distance as a narrow, bright crescent. This view is from the Jemez Canyon Overlook. Photo by John V. Young.

11

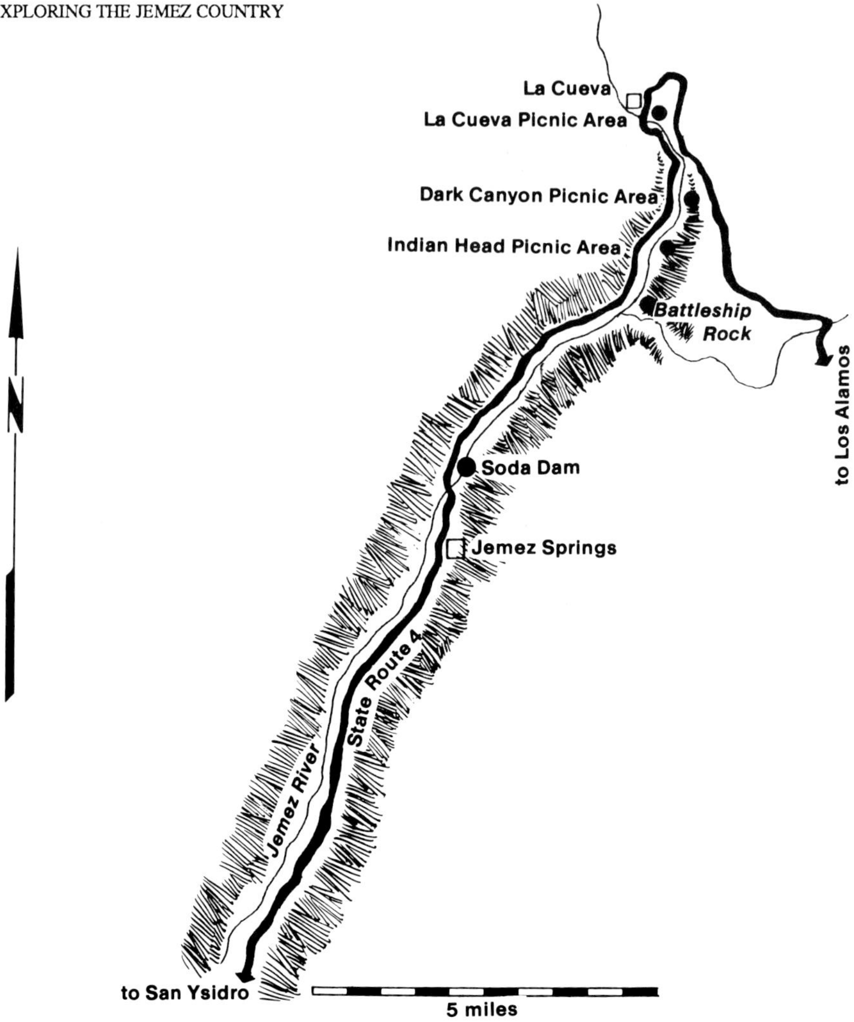

La Cueva
La Cueva Picnic Area

Dark Canyon Picnic Area

Indian Head Picnic Area

Battleship
Rock

to Los Alamos

N

Soda Dam

Jemez Springs

State Route 4

Jemez River

to San Ysidro

5 miles

Cañon de San Diego

As soon as you leave La Cueva junction and head south on State Route 4 toward Jemez Springs, there is a distinct change in mood and feeling. The montane meadows of the Valles caldera and the forested slopes of Banco Bonito have been left behind. New colors and smells intrude almost immediately on the senses, foretelling of new experiences waiting in the next 20 miles.

Like the prow of a ship, Battleship Rock stands regally over the confluence of the East and West Forks where they join to become the Jemez River. Battleship Rock was formed during the last eruptions of the Jemez Volcano. Photo by John V. Young

A Trench in Time

The red beds of the Abo Formation are exposed on the right side of the highway only a short distance from the junction. These are sedimentary beds of Permian age, deposited when New Mexico was covered by a shallow sea 280 million years ago. On the left-hand side of the canyon, across the river, are cliffs of black, iridescent obsidian. Occasional whiffs of sulphur from an abandoned sulphur mine near Hummingbird Music Camp drift in the wind, reminders of recent volcanic activity.

Along the three miles of stream from La Cueva junction to Battleship Rock there are three picnic areas, like jewels on a string of water. With mystical names like La Cueva, Dark Canyon, and Indian Head, they invite a pause beside the rushing stream. La Cueva Picnic Area has a fishing platform for the physically handicapped.

Battleship Rock

The rock that forms the pointed prow of the cliff named Battleship was one of the first volcanic flows to come out of El Cajete Crater. Long ago, the waters draining out of the lake in the Valles caldera had cut a deep canyon just to the east of the present Jemez River Canyon. Then the Battleship Rock flow poured down

13

Radiating cracks of the "rosette" of Battleship Rock resemble a torpedo hole at waterline. Photo by John V. Young.

this old canyon, completely filling it and displacing the stream to the west.

Look for the inward bulge at the base of Battleship Rock that resembles a torpedo hole at waterline. Called a "rosette" because of its radiating crack pattern, this peculiar feature is often found in igneous rocks having a columnar crack pattern. Rosettes occur at locations where igneous rock flows have solidified next to a cooler surface, as happened when the Battleship flow filled the older canyon.

A Remarkable Bit of Geology

Just north of the village of Jemez Springs is a geological phenomenon named Soda Dam. Technically speaking, it is a hot spring deposit of travertine rock that has been built from carbonated waters issuing from a fault zone. High on the west wall of the canyon can be seen the

remains of older "dams" formed long before the Jemez River cut down to its present level.

A fault zone crosses the Jemez River valley at this point and has thrust up the Precambrian-age granitic rock from deep below the surface. Hot mineral water, coming up along the fault, carried calcium carbonate in solution. When the water cooled at the ground surface, the minerals precipitated to form travertine deposits, which grew over thousands of years to create the structure now known as Soda Dam.

It is thought that the spring water at the dam is atmospheric in origin, consisting of surface waters which have been heated by circulating close to still-hot igneous rock. In contrast, the sulphur spring waters farther up the canyon are thought to be volcanic vapors still emanating from the magma chambers.

The pink granite cliffs by the side of the road just downstream from the dam are some of the oldest rocks in the world, nearly two billion

Untold generations of youngsters have worn out the seats of their bathing suits—or whatever they woro before bathing suits were invented—by sliding down the waterfalls through Soda Dam. This unique geologic structure lies beside State Route 4 just north of the village of Jemez Springs.

15

Fossils from the 300 million-year-old Pennsylvanian shale and limestone rocks are plentiful around Jemez Springs. Various types of crinoid sea-lily stems and corals are common finds.

years old—half the age of the earth. They have been thrust up from the underlying basement strata of the Rio Grande Valley and the Jemez Mountains. At the base of these cliffs, the youngest rocks in the world are being deposited every day as the hot waters continue to bubble up from below.

A Tale of Two Caves

Not only is Soda Dam a geological wonder, it was also an archaeological storehouse. For many years, stories were told of a dry cave under the dam, accessible only by an underwater passage. One of the valley's early settlers, Moses Abousleman, found the entrance and retrieved many Indian artifacts from it, including several handwoven blankets.

Another cave, more easily reached by less daring individuals, lies 100 feet above the dam on the west side of the canyon. Known as Jemez Cave, it was used by some of the earliest prehistoric human inhabitants of the valley. Its

occupancy dates from 2500 B.C. and continued through the early Spanish era. Indian artifacts from the cave include prayer sticks, rabbit clubs, and atl-atls. Also discovered was the mummified body of an Indian baby, wrapped in a blanket woven from a single 320-foot-long strand of twisted turkey feather down. Corn kernels from the cave, some of the oldest in the country, date to 880 B.C.

The printing on this stone reproduction of a road map is backward and must be read with a mirror, but that would suit our stone-age friend, Fred Flintstone, just fine, as he was kind of a backward guy himself.

A Modern Fossil

Indications have also been found that Fred Flintstone may have invented the first Xerox machine right here at Soda Dam. One day when Dave Owens of Los Alamos was visiting the area near the dam, he observed some highway crews cleaning out the road ditches near the dam where the hot springs run. As the maintenance crews pried out chunks of the calcium carbonate rock to deepen the ditches, one of the chunks split open to expose the imprint of a map.

17

Inspection revealed that it was a portion of a road map of Wisconsin, showing cities along U.S. Route 16 and Interstate 94 westward from Whitefish Bay, just north of Milwaukee. The larger cities of Menomonee Falls, Watertown, and Beaver Dam were clearly discernible, as well as a number of smaller towns and hamlets. The colors of the original map were also perfectly preserved, with the reds and blues of the highway system showing clearly.

It was speculated that the road map blew out of a passing tourist's car and landed in a little hot springs pool beside the road. The map sank to the bottom of the pool and was gradually covered with a deposit of calcium carbonate rock that precipitated from the spring water. In a year or so, the paper dissolved, but the ink stained the rock to leave a perfect copy of the original—in truth, a modern fossil.

Among the Ancient Ones

Two miles south of Jemez Springs, a tailings pile and weathered headframe mark the portal of the old Spanish Queen copper mine. Here in 1931, paleontologists from the National Museum of Natural History found the first fossilized skeleton of a Permian-age reptile, *Sphenacodon ferocior*. This animal, living 280 million years ago, was 9 feet long, weighed nearly 300 pounds, and was the most powerful carnivore of its day in New Mexico. Seashells from this period, fossilized by copper-bearing solutions that turned them into green malachite and blue azurite minerals, can be collected from a nearby tailings pile below the mine entrance.

An Unfolding Christian Pageant

Christianity has been a part of life in northern New Mexico since the first Spanish arrived.

Missionaries who accompanied Oñate to New Mexico tried to Christianize the Jemez Indians in 1598 and 1601. They attempted, unsuccessfully, to build a small adobe church at the prehistoric pueblo of Giusewa (Place of Boiling Waters) just north of Jemez Springs. A mission church was built at Zia Pueblo in 1614, giving that village the distinction of having the first permanent church in the upper Rio Grande Valley. In 1621, the mission of San Jose de los Jemez was built at Giusewa. It served until 1630, when the religious center for the valley was moved to Jemez Pueblo. The ruins of this old mission church at Giusewa are now within the boundaries of Jemez State Monument. Appropriately, the word *jemez* is the Spanish version of the Tanoan Indian word *hay-mish* meaning "people."

In 1878, a Presbyterian medical missionary, Dr. J. W. Schields, established the Presbyterian Church at Jemez Springs. He built a combination home and office across the roadway from the old mission ruins. In 1921, the Schields' home was sold and then enlarged to become a famous resort hotel, catering to a worldwide

The modern chapel of Via Coeli and the ruins of the Spanish mission of San Jose de los Jemez both have their foundations in the prehistoric Indian pueblo of Giusewa. The structure of each succeeding culture is almost exactly 300 years younger than the one that existed before.

19

clientele that came to enjoy the hot springs and the scenery. In 1947, Father Gerald Fitzgerald purchased the inn, converting it into a retreat house to provide spiritual renewal for overworked Catholic priests.

Father Fitzgerald founded two new ecclesiastical orders—Servants of the Paraclete (Holy Spirit) and Handmaidens of the Precious Blood. A new, strikingly beautiful, modern chapel called Via Coeli has been built across the road from the state monument, its foundations resting on the stones of the prehistoric pueblo. In 1972, the old inn-retreat buildings were condemned and demolished. The following year, a new retreat structure was built, again dedicated to spiritual renewal.

The Way to Heaven

Just as Christianity is dedicated to rebirth, so nature in the Jemez Valley also provides a second chance to view her fall loveliness. Several weeks after the aspens have turned gold at the higher elevations, the cottonwoods along the Jemez River take on their fall colors. When seen against the red cliffs, their yellow is especially vivid. Two miles north of Jemez Pueblo, the red sandstone rocks are sculptured to form a mini-combination of Bryce Canyon and Canyon de Chelly. Here in September, there is an especially beautiful display of emerald juniper, wild yellow daisies, and purple asters.

With scenery like this, one can't help but think that Via Coeli (Latin for "The Way to Heaven") is an appropriate name for the chapel that sits by the roadside in this valley.

Lichens form multi-colored patches on the shaded sides of rocks. This fortunate marriage of alga and fungus creates an organism that causes the breakdown of rock into soil. Photo by John V. Young.

Liken Your Life to the Lichen

Lichens are the result of a fortunate marriage of fungi and algae that began about 350 million years ago when the first plants established a foothold on dry land. Since then, they have covered the earth and helped shape it into what it is today.

A fungus and an alga coexist on the same small piece of rock by symbiosis—two organisms living together in a mutually beneficial association. For the partnership, the fungus, which secretes acids to dissolve the rock, scavenges minerals and stores water. The alga, which contains chlorophyll, photosynthesizes the raw materials into food for both partners.

For a wash-and-wear, easy-care pet, bring home a lichen-covered rock. Place it in a semiporous ceramic dish where you can see him and enjoy her. (Lichens, like many other plants, are bisexual.) They also enjoy companionship. So, give her a name and talk to him. Every week or so, place your friend and the container out in the sun or rain for a day. Your lichen will continue to live out the centuries until the rock is

21

completely digested and then it will start to work on the container.

The host rock for your lichen was blown out of a volcano in New Mexico about 1.5 million years ago and, except for the lichen colony, has remained relatively unchanged since that time. The age of your lichen colony has been estimated as being older than 10,000 years, possibly as old as 50,000 years—making it far older than any other single living organism.

Lichens, like humans, are among the world's hardiest and most adaptable creatures, being extremely resistant to temperature and humidity variations. However, they are very sensitive to air pollution and have been used to monitor the distribution and severity of airborne pollutants, particularly sulphur dioxide.

If your lichen should die, the best funeral that you could give him would be to send the remains (collect postage, of course) to your local or state government official. Include a note explaining that the cause of death was excessive air pollution and asking the official to clean up the environment to stop the murder of these unique organisms.

If your pet stays healthy, you'll have a living creature that has existed in its present form since the world was young, an organism that can adapt to almost any natural climate, and is composed of two dissimilar life forms that live in harmony for their mutual benefit. There is a lesson here for mankind. Come on people, if the lichens can do it, so can we!

WHERE MOUNTAINS CHANGE

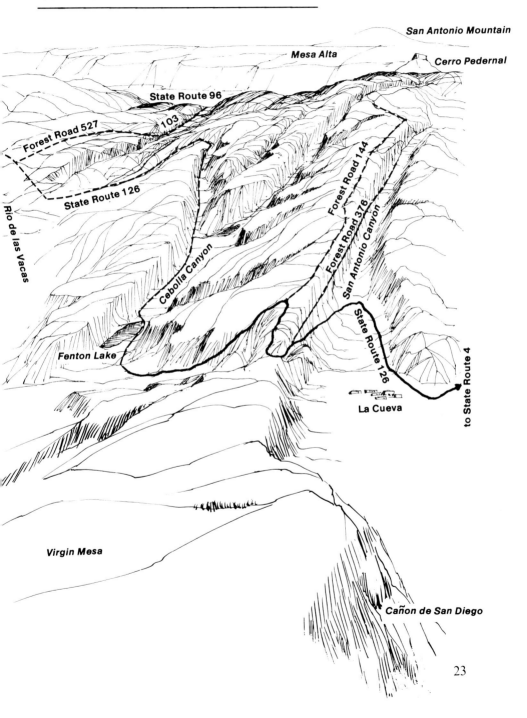

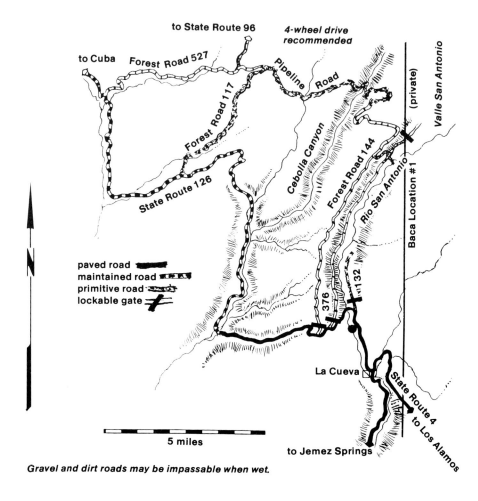

to State Route 96

4-wheel drive recommended

to Cuba   Forest Road 527

Forest Road 117

Pipeline   Road

(private)

Valle San Antonio

Cebolla Canyon

Forest Road 144

State Route 126

Rio San Antonio

Baca Location #1

paved road
maintained road
primitive road
lockable gate

132

376

La Cueva

State Route 4

to Los Alamos

5 miles

to Jemez Springs

Gravel and dirt roads may be impassable when wet.

San Antonio

What place in the Jemez Mountains has hot and cold running water, its own built-in air conditioning system, red carpets, and blue spruce-panelled walls? Plus special features for handicapped persons. Also fresh wildflowers every single summer morning.

No—it's not a motel, nor a plush dude ranch.

It's a canyon. San Antonio Canyon, to be exact. And in it flows beautiful San Antonio Creek.

This stream has its gentle beginnings in the cradle of the Valle San Antonio, the northernmost of the several valleys that make up the Valles caldera. San Antonio Creek, meandering through the meadows of its own private valle, drains the whole northern half of the Baca Location and includes the waters from several hot springs. It flows west out of the Baca property, then turns south through the deep and colorful San Antonio Canyon.

At La Cueva, the road junction of State Routes 4 and 126, San Antonio Creek joins with Sulphur and Redondo Creeks to become the West Fork of the Jemez River. A popular Forest Service campground is located in the lower end of the canyon along State Route 126, within two miles of La Cueva.

San Antonio Campground features a section specially constructed for use by handicapped persons. Paved paths are provided for wheelchair travel. There is a circular fire pit with a paved apron so that the handicapped can be wheeled close. Along the stream is an elevated ramp to provide an easy fishing spot for the physically handicapped.

Although there were several St. Anthonys in the history of the Catholic Church, the early Spanish settlers of New Mexico favored St. Anthony of Padua, Italy, as a patron saint when naming places. Brother Anthony, who was a personal disciple of Saint Francis of Assisi, began his career as a kitchen helper in the monastery at Padua where the lawyers for the Franciscan Order were trained. As a novice, he was ordered to give a sermon on short notice; he did it so successfully that he eventually became one of the most influential preachers of the Order. It is this same St. Anthony that is revered as a finder of lost articles.

The beauty and serenity of San Antonio Creek shine at every bend and riffle.

The Canyon Upstream

The real wonder and beauty of San Antonio Canyon lie upstream of the campground. The upper canyon can be explored in two ways—by footpath up the east side or by car up the west side.

Just before State Route 126 crosses the creek above San Antonio Campground, Forest Road 132 leads upstream. This dirt road, which dead-ends after two miles, provides partial access up the east side. Pretty little campsites along the way lure many a family into stopping, but it's worth driving to the end of the road and hiking up the canyon for another two miles.

An easy trail leads from the road through a mixture of tree groups and thickly grassed, open woodlands. This unspoiled setting of tumbling stream, boulders, heavily wooded canyon walls, trees, grass, and wildflowers is almost too perfect to be true. Yet it proves once again that perfection can be found in nature's randomness.

Ice Caves and a Red Carpet

About a mile north of the end of the road, a very shallow but steep canyon enters San

Antonio from the east. This is Ice Cave Canyon, named for the caves that supposedly are found here. Actually, the caves are no more than vertical crevasses in piles of huge boulders. The area is very difficult to explore because of the steepness of the slope and the profusion of thick brush on the hillside.

Snow evidently drifts into the openings between the boulders and remains as ice into early summer. Some of these openings are vented farther down the hillside at the bottom of the boulder pile, allowing for air circulation through interconnecting subsurface chambers. The air that drains out of these lower openings is chilled by contact with the underground ice and gives the effect of a natural air-conditioning system. It issues from the vents at about 45 degrees Fahrenheit, coming out with enough force to blow pine needles several inches away from the openings.

Farther up the canyon, the red beds of the Permian-age rocks are exposed. Uneven erosion has caused the valley floor to dip down occasionally into these lower strata, and the soil becomes brick red. It is here also that the large stands of magnificent blue spruce trees begin to appear. At one point it seems as if the trail is a red carpet extending down a long corridor lined with blue spruce.

By the West Road

About three-quarters of the way up Fenton Hill, Forest Road 376 heads off to the right and along the west side of San Antonio Canyon. The road follows the side of the canyon 800 feet above the creek and provides some spectacular vistas of the southern Jemez country. Along the edge of the canyon, purple asters nod in the breeze beside brilliant yellow daisies. Adding contrast are white yarrows and scarlet penstemons, plus orange-colored mallows. The wild

A pool in San Antonio Creek mirroring the volcanic tuff cliffs provides an idyllic setting for the perfect campsite.

raspberries usually fruit late in the fall, but the bountiful supply more than makes up for their tardiness.

After several miles, the road descends to the valley floor and follows close to the creek. All the varied beauty of the Jemez Mountains is present along this part of the canyon. Volcanic tuff cliffs line the road on the west; sharply pointed tent rocks march out into the meadows; then the canyon walls retreat to form a typical grassy Jemez valle.

Passage up San Antonio Canyon ends at the Baca Land and Cattle Company fence, nearly eight miles from the highway. Here, Los Alamos is only 40 miles and about an hour away.

It's easy to forget that this refreshing playground of natural beauty is quite close to home.

To the Pipeline Road

Those with a sense of adventure and 4-wheel drive can continue from here into the heart of the mountains. About six and a half miles up the canyon, unimproved Forest Road 106 branches off to the west and circles up the canyon wall to join Forest Road 144. The latter provides access to a large section of the northwest Jemez. To the south it loops back to State Route 126 through the woods and glens along the ridge top. Intriguing side roads lead off to the west and there are impressive views down Bear and Barley Canyons.

A wind-tortured conifer, clinging to the top of a cliff, signifies the universal will to survive.

To the north, Forest Road 144 runs along the rim of Cebolla Canyon and eventually intersects Pipeline Road. (The natural gas pipeline comes from Farmington, cutting across the Jemez Mountains to Los Alamos and the Española Valley.) From here Forest Road 144 turns east heading toward the spruce and aspen forest between Tschicoma and Polvadera Peaks. It ends, about 65 miles and many hours later, at the sawmill in Española.

Pipeline Road follows the pipeline westward, dropping precipitously down into and scrambling out of Cebolla Canyon. A pause at the rim provides a nice view down over the cliffs to the ribbon of the creek far below. The pipeline itself is exposed here as it plunges into the 800-foot canyon, an almost heroic man-made object in this wild land. Proceeding farther to the west, through the upper reaches of Calaveras Canyon, through open woodlands and past rustic high-country ranches, the Pipeline Road connects with Forest Road 117 at Moon Canyon and Forest Road 527 at Rock Creek. From here Forest Road 103 leads north amidst the high mesas and wooded hills into the Rio Puerco and San Pedro Parks country.

29

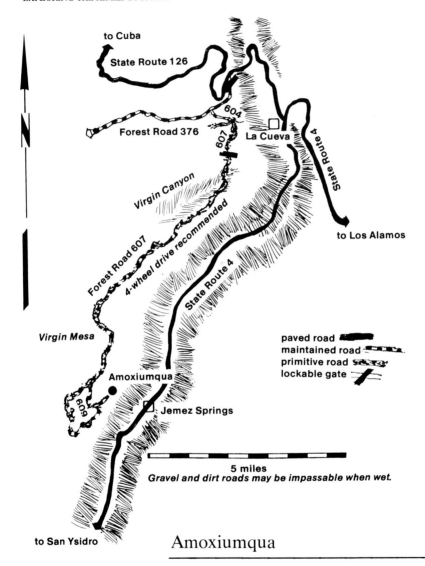

to Cuba

State Route 126

604

Forest Road 376

607

La Cueva

State Route 4

to Los Alamos

Virgin Canyon

Forest Road 607

4-wheel drive recommended

State Route 4

Virgin Mesa

Amoxiumqua

609

Jemez Springs

paved road
maintained road
primitive road
lockable gate

5 miles
Gravel and dirt roads may be impassable when wet.

to San Ysidro

Amoxiumqua

Take an Indian ruin, mix it up with moonlight and wildflowers and pine trees, and you get some typical New Mexico magic.

It's my conviction that camping at Indian ruins should be done during the time of a full moon. My formula is to explore the ruin in the daylight and then spend some of the moonlit hours trying to capture a feeling for the bygone greatness of the prehistoric civilization. At these times, it seems as if the spirit and personality of

the former inhabitants, who had such an infinite affinity for their own environment, come through more easily into the realm of our existence.

Sitting among the ruins, bathed in the ghostly moonlight, hearing the coyotes howl in the distance, listening to the sounds of the night birds, gives me a feeling of kinship with the past. I've always had a comfortable awareness that I was among friends, that I wasn't an intruder, but rather a welcome guest in the homes of the ancient ones. Such were the conditions when we made our first acquaintance with the Virgin Mesa ruins. It was the weekend of the full moon during the beginning of the Indian summer—a perfect time for camping in the Jemez country.

"He will set me high upon a rock...." This line from Psalm 27 comes readily to mind when sitting on the edge of Virgin Mesa overlooking Cañon de San Diego.

"Keep Taking Left-Hand Turns"

Virgin Mesa rises on the west side of the Cañon de San Diego. The mesa stretches for 12 miles, extending through three life zones, from its northern end near La Cueva to the southern tip at the confluence of the Rio Guadalupe and the Jemez River.

31

The large ruin of Amoxiumqua lies on top of this mesa due west of the village of Jemez Springs. A trail leads up the cliff from Mooney Boulevard behind the general store in the village, but it's a long, hard climb. On that particular weekend, Mary, Jeff, and I decided we would try to find the ruin from the maze of dirt roads that winds over the wooded hills and valleys between Lake Fork Canyon and the Jemez River. When we asked an old-timer how to get to the ruin, he gave what seemed to be an indefinite answer, but actually proved to be the only sensible reply in trying to describe directions. He said, "Just keep taking left-hand turns every time you can. Some will turn out to be dead ends, but back up and go ahead to the next left-hand fork."

Our first left turn was off State Route 126, about three miles west of its junction with State Route 4 at La Cueva. Here we turned south on Forest Road 376 toward Cañon. A mile down this road, we turned left again onto Forest Road 604. In yet another mile it was left once more onto Forest Road 607, which eventually led us down Virgin Mesa toward Amoxiumqua.

About five miles in from the pavement, still on Forest Road 607, we started down into Virgin Canyon. The remains of an old logging camp were just off the road at the upper end of the canyon. Several half-tumbled-down log cabins and a barn were all that was left of Chacer's Camp, named after two brothers who were logging contractors for the White Pine Lumber Company in the 1920s. According to Moises Sandoval of Jemez Springs, crews from this camp skidded logs by means of two-wheeled, horse-drawn wagons down to the railhead of the Santa Fe Northwestern Railway at Porter's Landing on the Rio Guadalupe. Operations from Chacer's Camp lasted from 1922 until 1929, when the lumber company ran into financial difficulty.

A mile or so farther on, the road climbed out

of Virgin Canyon onto Virgin Mesa. Occasionally, little spurs turned left off Forest Road
607 and went out to the canyon edge overlooking the Cañon de San Diego. We followed our
guide's advice to the letter and found these were
literally dead-end roads in the grimmest sense
of the word. We joked how dead you'd be if you
went over the end.

The overlooks provided some magnificent
views. From one of them, we could see Soda
Dam on the canyon floor more than 2,000 feet
below. Up and down the long sweep of the valley, the colorful red sandstones glowed through
the green conifers.

Stone bricks carved from the volcanic tuff of the Jemez Mountains were the building blocks for homes of the ancient Anasazi.

Clue to Past Glory

Forest Road 607 continued south along the
mesa top, passing small one- or two-room
Indian ruins as well as a few dilapidated log
cabins. Ten miles in from the pavement, we

33

Tall ponderosa pines crown the Jemez Mountains and shelter their wildlife. The cinnamon-colored bark of large trees has a distinct, vanilla-like odor. Photo by John V. Young.

turned left on Forest Road 609 near a sheet-metal rain-collector stock tank. Within a few hundred yards we took the final left-hand turn. Close by, on the highest point in the locality and about a quarter of a mile from the cliff edge, we found the ruin of Amoxiumqua.

It's unusual to find ruins among the ponderosa pines, but this pueblo seemed to belong among such stately trees. Today, it is only a large, grassy, rubble-strewn mound in an open space in the forest. However, its dimensions give a clue to past glory.

The pueblo was built in a rough H-shape, with the central spine nearly 350 yards long and with a north-south orientation. The two end wings were 200 yards long, 10 to 15 rooms wide, and two to three stories high. Within the west-

ward facing arms, a large water reservoir, 150
feet in diameter, was scooped out of the rock
and lined with clay. Seven kivas were constructed, the largest 35 feet across. Along the
southern side, three distinct levels can be seen,
as if there were three stair-stepped plazas.

A small amount of excavation was performed
here in 1911 by the Royal Ontario Museum of
Canada, and a few walls are still exposed from
that dig. It is thought that two periods of occupancy of the pueblo occurred, the first from
1300 to 1500 A.D., another—a brief one—during
the early Spanish era. The Franciscan friars in-
stituted a reduction program among the outlying pueblos to bring the Indians in closer to the
churches. As a result, Amoxiumqua was probably abandoned by the middle 1600s. Shards of
the well-known Jemez black-on-white pottery
litter the ruins. After all these years, the color
and sheen of the shards still make them look
almost like waxed egg shells.

We left these gemlike bits of shards and chips
amidst the grasses that clothe the ruins, wanting
other visitors to admire the fragile and frag-
mented beauty. We knew too that they would
someday provide archaeologists with valuable
information about the ancient ones who
fashioned vessels from the clay of this majestic
mesa. Others have felt as passionately as we the
need to protect all remains of the past. Our own
premier New Mexican archaeologist, Edgar L.
Hewett, wrote and guided through the U.S. Congress one of the wisest laws of the land. The
Antiquities Act of 1906 affirms the value of
these treasures and assesses stringent penalties
on those who would disturb them.

As we sat on the topmost part of the ruin that
night, an astonishing view of the lights of Albuquerque was spread out below. We guessed that
the ancient inhabitants of Virgin Mesa must
also have looked down in their time to view the
flickering fires of the pueblos along the Rio
Grande.

Mountain Mahogany

A most amazing plant—the mountain mahogany bush. This fuzzy-tailed friend is living proof that the wonders of the Jemez Mountain country aren't strictly limited to geological and archaeological features. Through the centuries, this bushy shrub has been a vital link in the chain of life's necessities for both humans and wildlife. In the Southwest, it has been one of man's best friends, used for a surprising variety of purposes.

Mountain mahogany is a native of the ponderosa pine forest, growing on sunny hillsides between elevations of 5,000 and 8,000 feet. Although most of the bushes are 6 to 8 feet tall, they sometimes grow to heights of 12 feet. Rather inconspicuous in the spring and summer, the mahogany comes into its full glory in the late fall when the fruit ripens and the seeds mature. It is aptly called "feather bush," for when the low morning or afternoon sun shines through the fuzzy seed pods, the bush appears to be covered with white feathers.

The botanical name for mountain mahogany is *Cercocarpus montanus*, which is a combination of two Greek words: *kerkos*, meaning "tail," and *karpos* for "fruit." That term doesn't quite adequately describe the wonderfully curly tail that sprouts when the blossom matures. Ruth Ashton Nelson, in her *Handbook of Rocky Mountain Plants*, says it in the fancy language of the botanist: "The flowers are without petals and the one pistil ripens into a pubescent achene with a conspicuously twisted and plumose tail, 3 to 4 inches long."

Strangely enough, mountain mahogany is a member of the rose family. The name mahogany was applied because the wood is so heavy. The early Spanish settlers in the Southwest knew it by the name *palo duro*. Because of its hardness, the branches were used by the Indians for arrow shafts and fish spears.

Big Medicine

The medicinal values of mountain mahogany are myriad—name the ailment and *Cercocarpus* can cure it. The Tewa Indians dried and pulverized the entire young plant, then mixed it with water for a laxative. Tea made from the bark induced perspiration and was said to be good for colds, even into the pneumonia stage. For cuts, the dry bark was powdered and used as a dressing to promote rapid healing. The inner bark was boiled and used as an eye wash.

The Spanish claimed that a decoction made from the leaves and drunk before breakfast was good for heart disorders. The inner bark—scraped, dried, and boiled—was excellent for lung trouble. This mixture, if taken long enough, was reputed to cure even venereal disease.

The inner bark was also an early source of red and purple dye used by the Navajos in their woolen blanket designs. Settlers found that the leafy twigs placed around a bedstead would keep the bedbugs away. Likewise, dried leaves under the mattress served the same purpose.

The wonderfully curled, spiral tail of the mountain mahogany fruit caused the early settlers to name it "feather bush."

37

Nature's Corkscrew

In spite of all the wide and varied uses of mountain mahogany, the most fascinating thing about the plant is the seed itself. One of the best examples of nature's amazing handiwork, it is perfectly engineered to do its job of propagating the species. Upon maturity, the seed is a fuzzy corkscrew, somewhat like a pig's tail. At the lower end is a streamlined bulge, which contains the actual seed kernel. The tail is only the transportation and planting mechanism.

In the fall and winter, the seed sits loosely in a little cup at the end of its twig, waiting for a breeze. The feather-like tail acts as a sail, catching the wind and allowing the seed to be carried out, up, and away.

The tail is covered with tiny white hairs, standing straight out from the central spine. When these hairs become wet, they lie back flat against the spine, causing the tail to straighten. Thus, when the seed lands on the ground and absorbs moisture, the tail begins to uncurl. In so doing, there is a tendency for the seed kernel to screw itself right into the humus of the forest floor. When the tail dries out, the curl comes back and the little hairs are extended again, acting as barbs against the seed being pulled out of its resting place. Subsequent wetting cycles will straighten the tail again, pushing the seed in deeper.

A most extraordinary plant—that mountain mahogany bush.

Food and Cover Crop

For hunters past and present, the bush is an indication of local deer and elk population. The leaves, twigs, and seeds are an important "winter-over" feed for these animals. During the spring and summer, when other food is available, deer and elk ignore mountain mahogany.

But for the remaining seven or eight months, it is a mainstay of their diet.

Deer will strip the leaves and new shoots from the bushes (often standing on their hind legs to reach higher), creating a definite "browse line" around the clump. Above this line the bush will be in full leaf, with the limbs stripped clean below. A mountain mahogany bush that has leaves and seeds from top to bottom is a good sign that the deer are somewhere else.

The Forest Service considers mountain mahogany an important reforestation crop, planting it liberally in timber sale areas. Several large, naturally growing patches of mahogany, perhaps a total of 200 acres, occur on Pinabetal Mesa on the north edge of the Jemez Mountains near Coyote. In October or November, the seeds are harvested by means of a vacuum cleaner from the back of a pickup truck. This one source provides the seeds for all Forest Service uses in New Mexico and Arizona.

Deer in the Jemez are ever alert to the passing parade of humans who intrude into their living space.

39

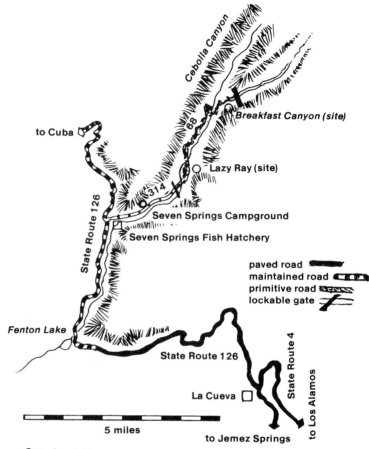

Gravel and dirt roads may be impassable when wet.

Cebolla Canyon

For nearly 50 years, an exclusive guest ranch operated in upper Cebolla Canyon. Over those five decades, the ranch achieved a reputation for both elegance and infamy—elegance because of its rustic refinement and infamy from the patronage of a Chicago gentleman named Al Capone.

Cebolla Canyon lies just west of San Antonio Canyon. State Route 126 to Cuba crosses the canyon at Fenton Lake, then turns north and

follows the Rio Cebolla for about four miles through an area of cabins and summer homes. Upstream of the settled region, eight miles of secluded beauty await the traveler.

Vertical silos at Seven Springs Fish Hatchery give a space-age look to the business of trout rearing.

From Egg to Creel

To reach this upper section of the canyon, turn off State Route 126 at the sign that points to the Seven Springs Fish Hatchery. The road goes right through the middle of the hatchery, where new ideas in trout raising are being developed to place more fish in the creels of New Mexican anglers.

Fish hatcheries are always fascinating places to visit. Seven Springs is particularly so for its natural setting, its history, and because—by means of a self-guided tour—a family can spend as much time as they want in a leisurely walk-through. Best of all, there's even a pond nearby to catch some of the fish that have been raised there.

41

Originally constructed in 1933, it is one of the oldest hatcheries in the state. The remodeling, which began in 1973, has transformed this site into a most modern trout producer. However, the building where the trout eggs are hatched is the original log cabin constructed over 40 years ago. It adds a typical New Mexican reminder of the past to the modern facilities.

In a unique development in the science of trout raising, a series of silos is used at Seven Springs. They consist of white plastic cylinders, 7 feet in diameter and 12 feet high, nearly completely buried in the ground. Water flows in a central pipe down the middle of the silo, then upward and outward to spill over the upper periphery. Each silo has a capacity of 3,500 gallons and can hold as many as 4,500 eight-inch-long trout. Feed is supplied continuously through electrically operated hoppers at the top of the silo. This combination of constant exercise, plenty of oxygen, and sufficient food makes for bigger fish at an earlier age.

It's worth stopping to take a look at the special show pond with the big fish. The sight of those red-sided submarines disguised as rainbow trout is guaranteed to raise the hackles on the back of the neck of even the most casual fisherman. Just up the canyon a short distance is a small lake called the Ice Pond which is stocked from the hatchery and is open to public fishing. Someday, somehow, one of the lunkers from the show pond might escape upstream to the Ice Pond and be waiting there to ambush the next baited hook that gets thrown in.

Up to Lazy Ray

Seven Springs Campground is a mile farther upstream. And this in itself is a pleasant surprise. Small but clean, and generally sparsely occupied, this campground has several sites right on the creek.

A short distance from a Forest Service gate, 1.2 miles above the campground, the road fords the Rio Cebolla, then heads upstream toward the Lazy Ray Guest Ranch a mile or so farther on. The floor of the canyon here is very flat and covered with waist-high grass. More than a decade ago, a beaver pond almost a third of the size of Fenton Lake covered the canyon bottom. A remnant of the dam can still be seen. But the pond filled in with silt and the beavers moved upstream.

The site of the old Lazy Ray is now barely discernible. All the buildings are gone; only a dozen or so blue spruce trees on the east side of the stream mark the location of the main lodge and dining room. Up a side canyon, a spring house high on a cliff still funnels water down to the nonexistent buildings.

In 1924, a Chicago advertising man named Seth Seiders built the Rancho Rhea (named for his wife) to entertain his eastern customers. Al Capone and his friends came to the ranch occasionally during the late 1920s, perhaps using the Jemez Mountains as a place to cool off when the climate became too hot in Chicago. In 1933, Ed "Tex" Thompson bought the ranch. In 1940, it was called Rancho Real by a new owner. Ray Craig then purchased it and changed the name to Lazy Ray Guest Ranch—a name that stuck until the end. In its day, the Lazy Ray was quite a place. Each guest room had a fireplace; there were also a large dining room, a lounge, a recreation room, and, on a terrace above the main lodge, a swimming pool. Across the creek, a bar and dance floor occupied a large log structure. Upstream a few hundred yards were the tack rooms, corrals, and wranglers' quarters. By 1970, because of increasing maintenance costs and a worn-out utility system, the ranch was no longer a profitable venture. The Forest Service bought the land and in 1972 razed the buildings, so that nature is once again in charge.

Over to Breakfast Canyon

From the Lazy Ray, the road leads upstream through grassy meadows on the west side of the canyon. It ends abruptly in about a mile, barricaded by a Forest Service berm. Just before this point, a side road fords the creek and winds over to Road Canyon. In the heyday of the Lazy Ray, this was called Breakfast Canyon. A quote from the ranch brochure describes it very well:

> One of the highlights of any week at Lazy Ray is the Sunday Morning Breakfast Ride. This trip takes you into Breakfast Canyon which is exceptionally beautiful with its silver spruce, quaking aspen shimmering in the early morning rays of the sun, clear and crystal springs and friendly wild turkey or scolding chipmunks. Chapel services are held with a ranch guest as the speaker or at times with a Minister or Priest from one of the churches of the area. The esthetic and intrinsic value of this gathering cannot be measured by any rule.

The old breakfast fireplace is still there, the crystal spring water still cascades down a rock face nearby, and the quiet magic hasn't departed. The surrounding volcanic tuff cliff faces are weathered into sharp spires giving the spot a cathedral-like quality.

Down along the Rio Cebolla, some eager dam-building beavers flooded out the old road that led downstream to the site of the dude ranch. The large ponds that were created hold both rainbow and German brown trout. Fishing in the beaver ponds was a popular recreation feature for the guests at the ranch. Now it's available to everyone and perhaps is even better than it was in the old days. Gooseberry bushes grow along the road, and the stream abounds with watercress plants. Although Cebolla Canyon was named after the flowers of the wild onion plant, a large variety of other wildflowers grow in the open meadows on the valley floor.

An hour's worth of trout from the Rio Cebolla. There are lots of fish to be caught, but it is a "hands and knees" creek. The rule is to keep out of sight and hook them on the first bite. Here, it's only one strike and you're out—of luck, that is.

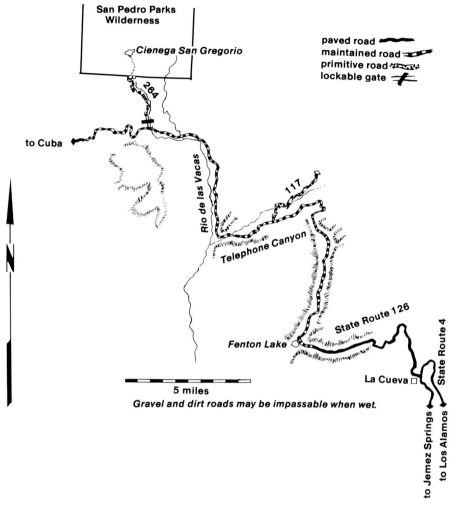

The Dirt Road to Cuba

State Route 126 to Cuba through the center of the Jemez country is paved from La Cueva almost to Fenton Lake. Then the road turns into dust, or to mud, depending on the season. Most likely it will all be a paved highway someday; but for now, I like it the way it is. (Probably the only people who can honestly make that statement are the ones who don't have to drive it every day.)

It's 33 miles from Fenton Lake across to Cuba, about an hour's trip in good weather if you drive straight through. Or it's a day-long trip, with time out for rock climbing, a picnic, and a hike into San Gregorio Lake.

Fenton Lake in winter is 30 acres of solitude.

When this road is dusty you can feel the geology between your teeth, or you can study the geology point-blank on your windshield when the road is muddy. It's possible to tell almost precisely when you travel out of the Jemez Mountain Range and start onto the Nacimiento Uplift just by the composition of the dirt on the road.

Where the Mountains Change

All the way to Telephone Canyon, eight miles past Fenton Lake, the road is built upon the volcanic rock of the Jemez Mountains. In Telephone Canyon a broad valley has been formed, with big blocks of volcanic tuff sticking up through the park-like meadows on the canyon

47

Los Alamos National Laboratory conducts research at Fenton Hill to study ways of extracting residual heat from the Valles caldera. Methods developed here are being tested elsewhere to use natural heat from hot, dry, rock formations. Photo by John V. Young.

floor. Green grass grows right up to the edges of the cliff faces, making it all look like a well-manicured playground. The scattered remnants of the volcanic tuff outcrops look as if they had been deliberately placed there as ready-made forts for small-fry cowboy and rustler battles.

Less than a mile past these outcrops, traces of red dirt begin to appear in the road. This part of State Route 126 occasionally dips down into the irregular surface of the underlying Permian red beds. When the road becomes red and muddy, it's a sign that you're traveling on the older, sedimentary beds that lie on the outer slopes of the Nacimiento Uplift. The side road that comes in from Moon Canyon on the north is often a mess of slippery mud, as these Permian-age mudstones literally turn into red grease when they get wet.

Where the road surface is sandy and well-drained, you know you're still on the Jemez volcanic tuff. Keep looking for the little shiny pieces of mineral that sparkle in the road when the sun hits them just right. These are fragments of sanidine crystals that weather out of the volcanic rock. When these bits of glitter disappear completely, you're no longer technically in the Jemez Mountains.

The Nacimiento Uplift

Fifty to sixty million years ago, some very important events began taking place in northern New Mexico when the Nacimiento ("birth" or "nativity") Mountains began pushing up. Twenty-five million years ago, the Rio Grande Rift started to open between the Nacimientos and the Sangre de Cristo ("blood of Christ") Mountains to the east, creating the broad valley of the Rio Grande. The eastern side of the Nacimiento Range slopes gently toward the rift. The western side of the range is much steeper because of an eastward dipping overthrust fault. The east side was thrust up as high as 6,000 feet above the west side.

Thick beds of shale and limestone had been deposited over this area in the seas of earlier ages during incredibly long periods of geologic time. When the region was pushed up, these sedimentary beds began to be eroded away from the granitic core in the center of the uplift. This granite is the same Precambrian rock underlying all of the Rio Grande country; the shales are the Permian red beds; and the limestones are of Pennsylvanian age. Outcrops of these same rock formations are also found in the Cañon de San Diego near Jemez Springs. Although shown on the maps as the Nacimiento Mountains, the range is geologically known as the Nacimiento Uplift.

On the Rio Grande side of the uplift, the sedimentary beds dip gradually toward the east. On the Cuba side, they dip steeply toward the west, except for a few places where the beds have actually been overturned by the Nacimiento Fault. In these localities the beds are either vertical or dip toward the east.

The Jemez Mountains, relative youngsters in geologic time, started forming 16 million years ago. The Jemez gradually built up through volcanic activity, leading to the dramatic series of eruptions that created the Valles caldera. The

creation of the caldera and the post-caldera eruptions, between 1 million and 130,000 years ago, represent only the last episodes in a long geologic history.

Rio de las Vacas

After the road to Cuba encounters the Rio de las Vacas ("River of the Cows"), it turns north to follow the meandering stream. As the road goes uphill, it cuts into lower sedimentary strata and is soon in the limestone beds below the red shale. On top of a little divide, a few limestone boulders lie among the ponderosa pines by the roadside. A close look at these rocks reveals embedded fragments of brachiopod shells and the disk-shaped columnar stems of crinoid sea-lilies. A mile and a half farther on, in a large open park near the stream, some of the first granite boulders from the core of the Nacimiento Uplift begin to be seen. Their rounded, exfoliated shapes give them the appearance of a cluster of giant eggs, and their pink and white variegated colors make you think immediately of the Easter variety.

San Gregorio Lake is a gem set in an inner circle of marshland enclosed by surrounding forest.

Cienega Gregorio

Two miles farther, Forest Road 264 to San Gregorio Lake leads north to follow Clear Creek. Bluebird Mesa rises just to the south, a high flat-topped, tree-covered area capped by the Chinle Sandstone formation. The road to the lake climbs rapidly; the conifers are mixed and so is the geology. Scab patches of sandstone, red shale, and limestone are seen among the trees. Right next to the road a little higher up, beavers have clogged the creek with a number of dams.

San Gregorio Lake is just inside the San Pedro Parks Wilderness Area. Vehicles have to be left in a Forest Service parking area, but from there it's only a half-hour walk in to the lake. At an elevation of 9,400 feet, the lake is situated within a wide ring of evergreens and aspens, set back to enclose a smaller inner circle of meadow grasses around the shore. It's also known by the name of Cienega Gregorio— meaning "marshy," for the marshland that surrounds part of it. The lake is actually a reservoir constructed to supply water to the Nacimiento

51

Community-Cuba Ditch. Always a popular
fishing spot, San Gregorio is stocked with
catchable-sized rainbow trout and cutthroat
fingerlings from the Seven Springs Fish
Hatchery.

And Down to Cuba

Back on State Route 126 and continuing west,
we see the vegetation changing toward the edge
of the uplift. Great patches of scrub oak cover
the hillsides, crowding out the pines. The road
descends the Nacimiento fault scarp by way of
Señorito Canyon and much of the complicated
geology is shown graphically in the cuts along
the downgrade.

Five miles east of Cuba, on the upthrown side
of the fault, is one of the oldest copper mines in
the country. Local historians claim that copper
was first mined and smelted by the Conquista-
dores, who conscripted Indian slaves to mine
the ore. Later, the deposit was worked in the
1880s. In 1917, there was a large mining camp at
Señorito. After World War I, the mine was
abandoned but production began again in 1971.
At that time the ore was excavated by bull-
dozers and hauled in 50-ton trucks. The ore was
processed by flotation at a maximum rate of
4,000 tons per day. The mine closed again in the
late 1970s. The ore deposit is in the Agua Zarca
("pure, clear water") Sandstone bed, the bottom
member of the Chinle Formation. The copper
ore is the mineral chalcocite, which has
replaced organic materials that were buried in
the sandstone. Some splendid petrified logs
more than 20 feet long have been found, with
the actual cell structure of the wood still visible.

LAND OF THE SPANISH SIGNS

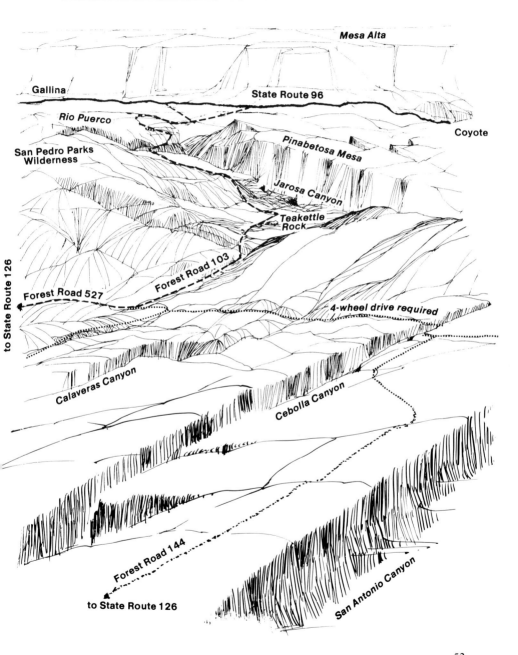

JEMEZ ASPENCADE

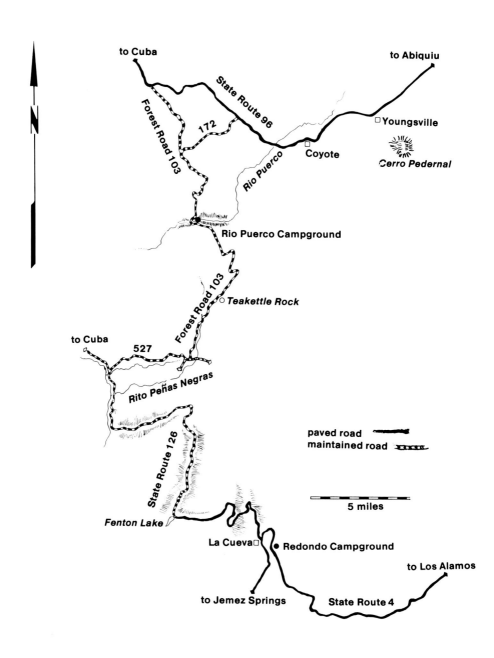

Gravel and dirt roads may be impassable when wet.

Jemez Aspencade

October is the time of year for the traditional family aspencade. Round up a crowd of friends, kids, or relatives. Take a picnic basket and a camera, and go off for a day of touring through the mountains. Store up in your mind all the beauty of a sparkling fall day in the Jemez. Let your senses become saturated with the riotous colors that nature has provided at summer's end.

When some friends from Kansas came for a visit, it seemed that such an expedition would be a good excuse to show off our mountains. (As if our family ever really needed any excuse to show off the Jemez country!)

The Northern Route

We picked a general route that would include the fabulous fall scenery around the Valle Grande, the northern mountain villages, and the spectacular red bed formations that lie on the edges of the Jemez. West towards Cuba, then north towards Gallina via the back roads, and return by way of Coyote, Abiquiu, and Española.

Our departure from Los Alamos that morning had been early—breakfast was to be at one of the Forest Service campgrounds along the way. By the time we reached Redondo Campground on State Route 4, everyone agreed that it was time to eat. Breakfast in the mountains just has to be cooked over an open fire. Somehow it all tastes better when mingled with wood smoke. Fried potatoes as only a Kansan can cook them, sausage, scrambled eggs with green chili, applesauce, warm doughnuts, and hot coffee made a glorious day even more so.

Later that morning as we drove by Fenton Lake, we almost weakened in our resolve to spend most of the day in the car. The blue

55

Golden-colored aspens make even rainy days bright with simulated sunshine.

waters extended an appealing invitation to just sit in the sun and look at the trees and the surrounding cliffs, but there were many miles of scenery ahead that needed seeing.

A mile north of Seven Springs Fish Hatchery, State Route 126 passes a pretty roadside picnic area near the entrance to Calaveras Canyon. The road then winds through groves of large aspen trees and climbs over a little divide before heading down Telephone Canyon. The ridge between the canyons is typical Jemez volcanic tuff rock—triangular tent shapes and deeply serrated cliff faces. Farther along, in the valley of the Rio de las Vacas, the road turns north. Here the canyon bottom is wider and the meadowland has been cultivated. Adobe ranch houses and rustic corrals look as much a part of the natural scene as do the rocky hillsides.

Rock Creek Road

About three miles before the turnoff to San Gregorio Lake, State Route 126 crosses Rock Creek. At the north bank, Forest Road 527 leads up the hill to the east. This well-graded byway first took us through open stands of ponderosa

When summer thundershowers hit, it's time to head for the nearest shelter, even if it is only the narrow arch of Teakettle Rock.

pine on Rock Creek Mesa; then we crested a hill and the vegetation changed abruptly. Down we wound through thickets of yellow locust bushes and clumps of still-green aspen. At the big meadows on the Rito Peñas Negras (Spanish for "Black Rock Creek"), we turned north on Forest Road 103. For three miles the road follows the sparkling creek up to its headwaters. Then we crossed a wooded ridge and started down into the drainage basin of the Chama River.

As Forest Road 103 continues north, the country changes drastically. Remnants of volcanic tuff remain only on the highest mesas. The valleys are cut down into the ancient sandstones that were deposited 200 million years ago in Triassic time.

The Teakettle Near the Rio Puerco

Just before we started down into Jarosa Canyon, Teakettle Rock appeared close beside the road. Set in open country near some cultivated fields, this landmark of the northern Jemez region cannot be overlooked. The unique sandstone formation is a natural "jungle gym"

57

—exploring the caves and tunnels under it is as much fun as climbing through the arch. Local legend claims that Pecos Bill used the pot to brew green tea. The green stains on one side of the formation stand as proof of this story, although some killjoys have been known to shrug the stains off as merely being copper deposits. As Rio Puerco means "muddy" or "dirty river," it's possible that some of the tea is still spilling out of the pot to discolor the creek down at the bottom of the hill.

The valley of the Rio Puerco is startlingly beautiful and quite different from typical Jemez country. The dense vegetation is mostly scrub oak; slabs and ledges of Chinle sandstone outcrop along the rim. The same red-bed formations that occur south of Jemez Springs also appear here in the side slopes. In the canyon bottom, the stream tumbles over boulders of older, light-colored fossiliferous limestone.

Rio Puerco Campground was a beauty spot in the upper part of this canyon, where we had intended to eat. That day it was closed and the entrance blocked. A Forest Service notice proclaimed that the campground was completely wrecked by vandals in 1972 and that money wasn't available for repairs. It seems inconceivable that it could have happened, because anyone who camped there could not help but love the place. (The Forest Service has since repaired the damage and once again campers can sleep and dream in this small, gem-like spot beside the rushing stream.)

Coyote, Pedernal, and Abiquiu

After traveling seven miles of dirt road past the Rio Puerco crossing, we came to State Route 96, the paved highway to Cuba that skirts the northern end of the Jemez Mountains. On it we turned eastward toward Coyote and Abiquiu Dam. This part of the drive is colorful in any

season, particularly so when the autumn hues intensify the richness of the rock formations. Interbedded layers of maroon and green shale are seen in some of the roadside cuts. Across the valley, the red- and white-layered cliffs of French Mesa stand against the sky. White gypsum boulders from the top strata spill down the hillside to lie in contrast on the red-colored lower slopes. The village of Coyote is a study in camouflage as the reddish-brown adobe walls blend in with the surrounding hills.

Always prominent on the skyline in this part of the Jemez is odd-shaped Cerro Pedernal. The horizontal flow of basalt that caps the mesa has been eroded to a long, narrow strip. When viewed from the headwaters of the Rio Puerco, it appears as a sharp-pointed peak. From the highway near Youngsville, it is seen as a flat-topped mesa. Several hundred feet below the summit occurs the 15-foot-thick layer of flint from which the peak gets its Spanish name of *pedernal*. The layer constitutes one of the

The distinctive profile of Cerro Pedernal (Flint Hill) dominates the skyline at the northeastern edge of the Jemez country. Long before the Anasazi arrived, prehistoric man dug flint from its slopes for arrowheads.

59

earliest mines in North America. Thousands of years before the beginning of the Pueblo culture, prehistoric man dug in the slopes of Pedernal Peak to obtain flint for projectile points. Numerous remains of quarries and camps of the Indians who sought the stone can still be found on the rocky side slopes.

Dazzling Autumn Tapestry

The highway crosses the top of Abiquiu Dam, completed in 1963 by the U.S. Corps of Engineers to control floods on the Rio Chama. The dam is an earthfill structure, 325 feet high, spanning a narrow spot in the canyon. From the road just beyond the dam, an impressive panorama of western "big sky" country is seen. All the multitinted cliffs of the Ghost Ranch and Echo Amphitheater areas form a frame for the Chama Valley. Here we turned south on U.S. 84 toward Española and home.

Halfway between the dam and the village of Abiquiu, there is a particularly good view of the Chama River. The highway seems to be encased by wrinkled red cliffs as it begins to drop down off the plateau. Then suddenly, like a window opening, the bank on the right disappears, and the great yellow cottonwood trees along the river banks below are seen in their full fall splendor.

On our special day, the colors of the cottonwoods lined the valley with their brightness all the way to Española. And the red chili ristras, seen hanging from adobe walls, added their own spicy flavor to the autumn glory of northern New Mexico.

The Crosses of the Jemez

Weather-beaten cross-
es in the *camposantos*
of mountain villages in
northern New Mexico
possess a peace and
dignity that belong to
another age.

"Adelante de la Cruz!" used to be the family
rallying cry when New Mexican fathers of two
generations ago were urging their children to
get ready to go to church, or to town, or even
out to do the chores.

"Forward with the Cross!" came to mean
"Hurry up, let's get moving" more than its
actual connotation of "Forward with the work
of the Lord." Whatever its meaning, it symbol-
ized how much the Christian cross had become
a part of the daily life of the people.

Jesucristo

In the mountain villages of today, this close
affinity with Christianity is still demonstrated
by the public display of the cross. Along the
roads and highways, on the hilltops and in
churchyards, crosses are erected for a variety of

61

specific reasons, but always for the same overriding purpose—to identify with *Jesucristo.* This is particularly true at Easter time, when additional crosses appear in the village *moradas.*

In the Spanish counties of northern New Mexico, Christianity has always been deeply rooted in the lives of the non-Indian people. This is rightly so, for most of them are of true Spanish ancestry and can trace their lineage directly to the early explorers and settlers. As the Spanish Crown supported the colonization of New Mexico for the sole purpose of bringing Christianity to this far-off land, it was only natural that the settlers themselves were deeply religious. The solitude and rigors of New Mexican living further intensified their religious feelings.

The Pueblo Indians took Christianity and made it uniquely their own, in spite of the way they were often mistreated and abused in its name. They accepted this new religion but also performed their own ancient rituals.

El Descanso

The crosses that are seen along the roads around the edge of the Jemez Mountains are erected by both Spanish and Indians alike for one of three reasons. The cross may mark a place where a person was killed in an automobile accident. In this case, the cross not only commemorates the location of the accident, but also marks the place where the spirit left the body. The cross may mark a place where a person was critically injured in an accident, although he may actually have died somewhere else. Finally, the cross may mark a place where a funeral procession rested. In the old days, pallbearers stopped to rest and erected a cross as they carried the coffin from the home to the graveyard called in Spanish *camposanto,* "holy field." Now, in the days of motorized funeral processions, a spot is chosen beforehand for the procession to pause and that location is marked with a cross.

The spot where a cross is located is generally called *el descanso* or "resting place"—the place where the spirit rested before leaving the body. In fact, the cross itself has now come to be loosely called a *descanso*. Today only the people of Spanish extraction put up crosses at the scene of highway accidents. The Pueblo Indians, on the other hand, have the exclusive tradition of stopping the funeral procession at a designated spot and of later erecting a cross in memory of the deceased at that location.

Los Hermanos

The week before Easter sees a marked increase in the activity of cross-raising in the Spanish villages. At that time, however, the crosses do not commemorate death, but celebrate life. All during Lent, men of the *Penitente* sect have been going to their village *morada* to pray and meditate. At the beginning of Holy Week, they retire to the *morada* to live. (The actual definition of *morada* is a "dwelling place" or "residence," but in northern New Mexico it generally denotes the building that the *Penitente* brotherhood uses as a base of operations.) Villagers jokingly say that you can tell when spring is near by the fresh tire tracks in the yards of New Mexico's *moradas*.

Until a generation ago, the *Penitentes* reenacted the complete story of Christ's crucifixion. Members were chosen to portray the characters in the Easter story, and they performed their parts with great enthusiasm—and often quite bloodily. Now few perform the rituals of whipping and self-inflicted punishment. Although details of the practices of the *Penitentes* may vary among villages, usually the same general form of worship prevails. The men put up crosses in the yard of the *morada*; they stay inside most of the time, praying and fasting. Families are chosen from the village to take food to them. In some localities, a sister sect—women known as *Carmelitas*—prepares and serves the food. On Holy Thursday and Good Friday, villagers are sometimes permitted to take part in the meditations in the *morada*. In one area near Hernandez, children used to walk and pray with a *Penitente* as he carried his heavy *madero* through the historic Stations of the Cross. The word *madero* translates literally as "heavy beam" or "timber," but locally it has come to signify the cross that Christ carried. Some people even equate the word with the load of sin mankind carries.

Women's Lib has not penetrated the *moradas* of northern New Mexico, nor is it likely to. The secret rites of the Brotherhood—*Los Hermanos* —are still closely guarded and visitors may see only a few outward acts of worship.

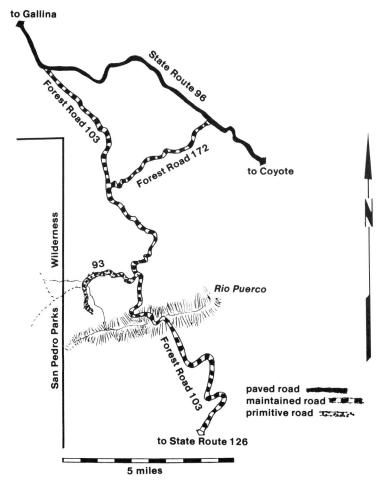

to Gallina

State Route 96

Forest Road 103

Forest Road 172

to Coyote

N

Wilderness

San Pedro Parks

93

Rio Puerco

Forest Road 103

paved road
maintained road
primitive road

to State Route 126

5 miles

Gravel and dirt roads may be impassable when wet.

San Pedro Parks

If you seek tranquility in your scenery, go to the northwest corner of the Jemez country on the northern edge of the Nacimiento Uplift. That's the address of the San Pedro Parks Wilderness Area, 70 square miles of quiet landscape. Here, there are no mountains rising to the sky asking to be climbed. Just gentle, rolling

65

Quiet, open meadows surrounded by low, forested mounds provide a peaceful change of pace in the San Pedro Parks Wilderness.

topography, two miles above sea level, characterized by large grassy meadows separated by low mounds on which dense tree groups grow. The wilderness is laced with meandering streams, deep, clear, with undercut banks where the shy native cutthroat lives.

The region was designated as a Primitive Area by the Forest Service in 1931 and became the San Pedro Parks Wilderness Area in 1965. As such, no vehicles are permitted, so it's strictly packhorse or back-packing country.

Beaver Country

The wilderness can be entered from almost any side. Good trails exist from a number of entry points. However, if you want to see beavers, camp by beaver dams, be amused by their antics, listen to them working in the moonlight, and have them sagely scrutinize your activities—then go in from the Rio Puerco on the east.

From State Route 96 between Gallina and Coyote, turn south on either Forest Road 103 or Forest Road 172. These merge and continue up the hill as Forest Road 103. At the top of the divide, pause and look east through the trees for a spectacular view of Cerro Pedernal. Across the road a very red and dusty Forest Road 93 turns to the west.

Forest Road 93 follows a stream about a mile on the outside of the wilderness boundary. Here are several active beaver colonies, with the animals usually visible in the mornings and evenings. A trail into the wilderness goes up the Rito Resumidero, translated roughly as "Repeater Creek" because it sinks out of sight and then reappears. Leading at first through heavy timber, the trail crosses numerous small *vegas* (meadows)—in each one is a beaver dam. At the head of Oso ("Bear") Creek, where the first large park begins, there are a huge dam and a pond, several acres in size. Within the wilderness, the beavers are relatively unafraid and can be seen with frequency. Before the day of the beaver trappers, it was said that the beavers worked day and night in their ponds, since the Indians regarded them as brothers and left them unharmed. San Pedro Parks furnishes an insight into what America must have been like in the days before the white man came.

The Land of the Spanish Signs

At first glance, it appears that all the signs within the wilderness area are written in Spanish. After hiking past several of these trail markers, you may well ask yourself, "What country am I in, anyway?" It's not that the signs are written in Spanish to confuse the Anglos, it's just that the names of all the features in the area are Spanish names. So the direction signs are really written in Spanish out of necessity.

A member of the lily family, skunk cabbage may grow 4 to 6 feet tall in moist mountain meadows.

The trails that cross the open parks are some-times hard to follow. In these places, rock cairns have been built, each with a wooden post stick-ing up. Hiking is like doing a child's dot-to-dot game. You proceed from one cairn to the next, not making any plans for direction until you see the next one.

The highest peaks are in the north-central part of the parks, along the Rio Capulin trail. A mound of rounded pink granite rock towers fully 50 feet above the surrounding meadows. And on top is a sign proudly proclaiming (in English this time), "San Pedro Peak, Elevation 10,502 feet."

Even the humor seems to be gentle in this wilderness.

The Summer Rains

It is not a capricious trick of nature that gives the Jemez country its summer rainy season to ruin the afternoon sun-bathing sessions. The daily thundershowers may seem like poor planning on the part of the weatherman, but at least there is a reason for them, as they are directly related to the geography and geology of the Jemez Mountains.

By early July, the large high-pressure area that has been riding over the Atlantic Ocean for most of the winter has moved west and north over the Gulf Coast. Winds that skirt the edge of this "high" move in a clockwise direction and bring warm, moist air sweeping up from the Gulf of Mexico. The eastern slopes of the Sangre de Cristos receive much of this moisture; however, there is a gap in the mountains south of Santa Fe and north of the Sandia Mountains through which the Gulf air can pass. This moist air then rises on the slopes of the Pajarito Plateau and drenches the Jemez in daily summer thundershowers.

As summer ends, the northern hemisphere begins to tip away from the sun, and the tropical cloud zone retreats southward, taking the Gulf Coast "high" with it. At this time, there is a cessation of the southeasterly winds. Several months of beautiful, warm Indian summer can be counted upon before the westerly winds start to bring cold, winter Pacific air sweeping down from the northwest across the Rockies.

Upslope Effects

The thundershowers and hailstorms characterizing the summer weather result from what are known as "upslope" effects. As moisture-laden air moves across the country, the presence

69

The rains of July and August bring out wild-flowers that often last into October. Here, golden-eye viguieras glow beside lavender fleabanes.

of mountains causes the air to rise as it goes upslope. An increase in altitude means a decrease in temperature, and as the air rises and gets colder, it is unable to hold as much moisture as it did at lower, warmer altitudes. When this happens, the air loses its moisture in the form of rain or snow.

Also significant in the making of storms are the elevation and eastern exposure of the Jemez Mountains. The steep slopes absorb the heat of the early morning sun, so that the warmed earth heats the upland air before the valley air is heated. The warm air begins to creep up the mountain sides, creating a morning breeze as it draws up replacement air from lower elevations. The heating of the air is further accelerated by reflection from the large areas of bare rock and sparse vegetation typical of the Pajarito and Jemez plateaus. The warmed air rises quickly, and the moisture in it condenses to form clouds over the mountains. In the summer, the freezing altitude is 14,000 to 16,000 feet. When clouds rise above these heights, they contain raindrops, snow or hail. During the warmer months, the snow turns to rain before it hits the ground; but the hailstones, being bigger and falling faster, do not have time to melt.

The cliffs and clouds combine for some spectacular summer vistas. The mounds of piled-up whipped cream make New Mexico's skies several shades bluer by contrast. On any July or August day, up to half the state enjoys thunderstorms. The Jemez area is so fortunately situated that it may receive two or three of these beauties a day; and Los Alamos averages 58 thunderstorm days a year with lightning or thunder, with or without rain.

The thunderclouds of summer pile like whipped cream over the Jemez Mountains.

A Home for the Gods

A thundershower often develops like this: At 10:00 a.m. on a typical July morning, there are only a few wispy clouds over the Jemez. By 11:00 a.m., the wisps have grown into tall cumulus clouds as the incoming moist air moves upslope on the outlying plateaus. A half hour later, the cumulus clouds have filled the western sky with their billowing whiteness. As their height increases, the bases begin to darken. At 12:15, the cloud bursts in an awesome display of nature's fury. It has grown into a full-fledged cumulonimbus type, with an anvil-shaped top of cirrus clouds. Great offshoots spread out like horns from its upper surface. Its base is black and often attains a width of five miles or more. Hanging from the leading edge of the storm are streamers of rain called "virga," raindrops that evaporate before they reach the ground.

When clouds like this are laced with lightning and boom with thunder, it is no wonder that the ancient Pajaritan people regarded them as a fitting home for Avanyu, their all-powerful, feathered-serpent diety.

71

Skiing the Jemez Country

Cross-country skiing has taken the Jemez by storm! Skiers experience the "peaceful exhilaration" of gliding through the silent, snowy woods.

It's probably a lousy pun to say that cross-country skiing has taken the country by storm. Or that every winter storm causes a new blizzard of interest in cross-country skiing. But pun or not, it's true. More and more people have found the thrill that comes from experiencing the solitude of the mountains in their velvet stillness.

To follow a ridgeline between mountain-tops, with nothing but deep blue sky above and a pristine world below, makes for pure joy of living! Paradoxically, the deep dead silence of the snow-smothered woods can provide its own mountain-top type of experience. "Peaceful exhilaration" might be the way to express it.

Northern New Mexico is proving to be a mecca for cross-country skiing. The Jemez country, with its open valleys and wooded mesas, is becoming very popular. A few inches of snow are all that is necessary to provide cover for a day's skiing on the forest roads that lead off from State Route 4.

On Preventing Sticking

At the altitude of the high Jemez, the sun warms the snow quickly, but the shaded areas remain quite cold, so you continually face drastically different snow and wax conditions—possibly every few yards. When the snow is soft and wet, even no-wax skis will start to stick. Here is the remedy for that. If the air temperature is above about 25 degrees Fahrenheit, give the bottom of the skis a coating of silicone spray before starting out. (Buy the silicone at the hardware store; it's cheaper than in the sporting goods store.)

At nearly any temperature, you can ski leisurely in the shaded areas. But on a warm day

when a sunny stretch of trail lies ahead, particularly a south-facing one, ski across it as fast as possible, and don't lift your skis up off the snow. Keep them sliding along in constant contact with the snow to prevent ice crystals from building up. Run, don't walk, to the nearest shade. Yes, it is exhausting, but after all, you are out there for the exercise and you will feel like an Olympic champion after that short dash. When you get to the shade again, don't stop immediately, but ski into the shade for 15 or 20 feet. This will give your skis a chance to come to temperature equilibrium and will prevent the moisture on them from freezing when they contact colder snow.

A blanket of snow silences the babble of the East Fork of the Jemez River in its cliff-lined box near State Route 4. The velvet stillness of the snow-covered Jemez attracts thousands of cross-country skiers each winter.

Disaster Prevention

Cross-country skiing deserves a few special precautions. *Never ski alone, or at least tell someone where you will be skiing and when you expect to return.* Carry a repair kit! Look over your bindings, skis, and poles carefully and decide

Fire roads branching from the Apache Spring picnic area invite cross-country skiers to explore.

how you would repair each part if it broke. Then pack a repair kit in a small stuff sack and take it with you every time. Trying to walk in deep snow for even half a mile can be exhausting. I was 13 miles away from my vehicle one time when my unbreakable binding broke. A 6-inch length of coat hanger was my salvation. (When I later contacted the manufacturers of my binding, they were amazed that such a thing had happened, but that didn't help me at the time.)

Also think of what you would do if the bale came off your ski pole. It could be much more serious than you would think. You don't realize how much you depend on those poles until you begin to sink up to the handle on each stride. Some useful items to carry in your repair kit include: Swiss army knife, small pliers, screw driver, tube of super glue, wire, tape, butane lighter.

Emergency Gear

Cross-country skiing is an activity that can turn into a disastrous situation in very short order—either from a sudden change in the weather or from an accident that extends the trip into a night-time nightmare. Carry at least three butane lighters—one in the repair kit, one in an outside pack pocket, and one in your pants pocket. In an emergency or during sub-zero weather, you don't want to fumble through your pack to find a lighter. The sustained mini-torch flame gets a fire going a lot faster than matches. A butane lighter is also an excellent tool for pinpointing heat to speed up the setting of super glue. (I have used super glue to reset screws in their holes after they have pulled out.)

Carry water in pint-sized containers. Since they fit inside your shirt, it is easier to keep them from freezing. Also, they are easier to thaw by body heat if they do freeze. Cut dense food, such as cheese, meat, and candy into bite-size pieces before starting out. Small pieces are much easier to thaw, or even to eat frozen, if you need a quick-energy recharge in a hurry. And take a container to heat water in, even if it is only a Sierra cup.

An extra pair of wool socks is essential. A balaclava doesn't take up much room in your pack, and it provides head and face protection at night during cold weather. You must keep your head warm enough so that the rest of the body can function. On extended trips, the party should take along at least one bivy sack (a light-weight, waterproof cover for a sleeping bag) or an aluminized "emergency bag." In a real emergency, three people in a bivy sack in a protected location have a good chance of surviving a sub-freezing night. This emergency gear all fits in a pack tossed in the back of the vehicle, ready to go in an instant.

75

Off to the Mountains and Mesas

Then off to the mountains where the powder awaits. If you haven't found your own secret run, several books list the better-known trails in the Jemez. Try Rincon Bonito Road north from the Los Alamos ski area and the Bandelier National Monument run near St. Peter's Dome Road. The New Mexico Ski Touring Club has marked trails at Peralta Canyon Road, at Las Conchas Trailhead, at East Fork Trailhead, and at Redondo Campground.

In very special years, when snow blankets the low mesas surrounding the caldera, try skiing the piñon-juniper woodland. The deep woods are a sterile and silent place in winter, but in the piñon country there is plenty of evidence of wildlife. Deer and elk winter at these elevations, coyotes hunt all winter long, and the tracks of rabbits and kangaroo rats are usually plentiful. There is also lots of bird life—juncos, chickadees, jays, hawks, and eagles.

The dirt roads east from State Route 4 between White Rock and Bandelier are leisurely runs. The vistas are magnificent through the low, scattered trees. Both the Sangre de Cristo and Jemez Mountains are in view—as are the broad Rio Grande Valley and the rim of White Rock Canyon. Moonlight skiing in the piñon country is especially enjoyable because of the scarcity of shadows. It is truly a rare experience.

THREE ROADS TO COCHITI

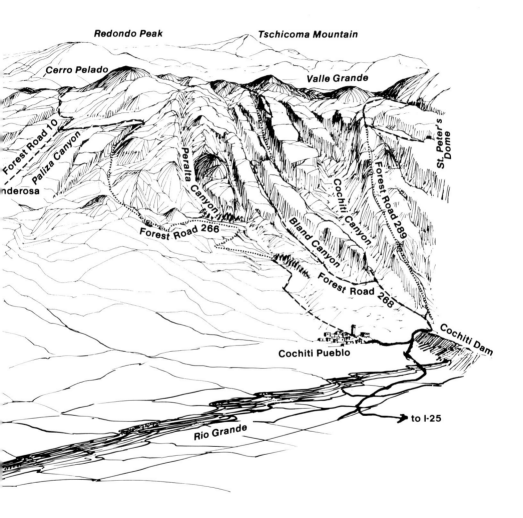

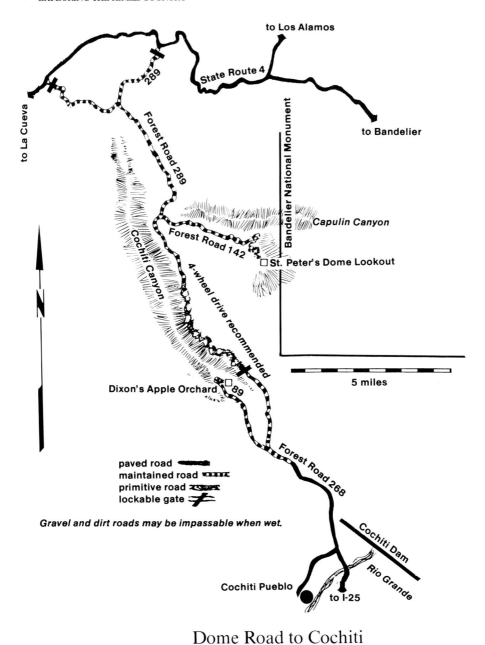

to Los Alamos

State Route 4

to Bandelier

289

to La Cueva

Forest Road 289

Bandelier National Monument

Capulin Canyon

Cochiti Canyon

Forest Road 142

4-wheel drive recommended

St. Peter's Dome Lookout

5 miles

Dixon's Apple Orchard 89

Forest Road 268

paved road
maintained road
primitive road
lockable gate

Gravel and dirt roads may be impassable when wet.

Cochiti Dam

Rio Grande

Cochiti Pueblo

to I-25

Dome Road to Cochiti

From State Route 4, there are three roads to Cochiti—high, middle, and long. They could easily be nominated for the best scenic drives in the state.

The fire tower at St. Peter's Dome commands spectacular views of the Bandelier Wilderness, Rio Grande Rift, and southern slopes of the Jemez Mountains.

The high road, Forest Road 289, is the most easterly of the three. Usually called the St. Peter's Dome Road, it leaves State Route 4 about 11 miles west of Los Alamos. The sign on the highway indicates that the Dome Lookout is 13 miles away and that Cochiti Lake is 23 miles away. There is an excellent, although unimproved, camping and picnic area just two miles in from the highway in a large, open meadow among the pines.

To St. Peter's Dome

A little over four miles farther on, the road to the Dome Lookout branches off to the east in a separate spur called Forest Road 142, while the main road continues down the ridge toward Cochiti. From the lookout road, several trails lead into the back country of Bandelier National Monument, putting Painted Cave and the Shrine of the Stone Lions each within a day's hike of transportation.

The lookout itself provides an unequalled view of the Pajarito Plateau. To the north, the columnar cliffs of Capulin Canyon and the

79

Ladybugs huddle in the groove of a yucca leaf. Such swarms of the colorful insects are one of the unimagined surprises of the Jemez Mountains, delighting lucky hikers who chance upon them.

spire of Boundary Peak are the most prominent close-in features. In the middle distance, Los Alamos, White Rock, the Rio Grande, and Bandelier are spread like a map on the floor. To the south, beyond the waters of Cochiti Lake, the green fields near Cochiti Pueblo stand out against the parched background. Immediately to the southwest, the alpine summit and scree slopes of Cerro Picacho ("Peak Hill") dominate the view.

At St. Peter's Dome, we once enountered one of the unimagined surprises of the Jemez Mountains, a swarm of ladybugs. The bushes around the lookout were covered with gallons of crawling red-and-black ladybugs. In late summer or early fall, after feasting on aphids in the lowlands, the colorful insects gather in large numbers on the mountain tops. They hibernate there in protected places until spring, when they fly back to the croplands for mating, egg-laying, and eventual death.

On to Cochiti

Forest Road 289 continues down to Cochiti along the narrow mesa between Sanchez and Cochiti Canyons, sometimes tipping precariously close to the latter. The view in places is almost frighteningly spectacular. After a hairpin turn past the old Eagle Canyon Pumice Mine, the road glides down through Eagle Canyon and south across the gentle hills toward Cochiti Lake.

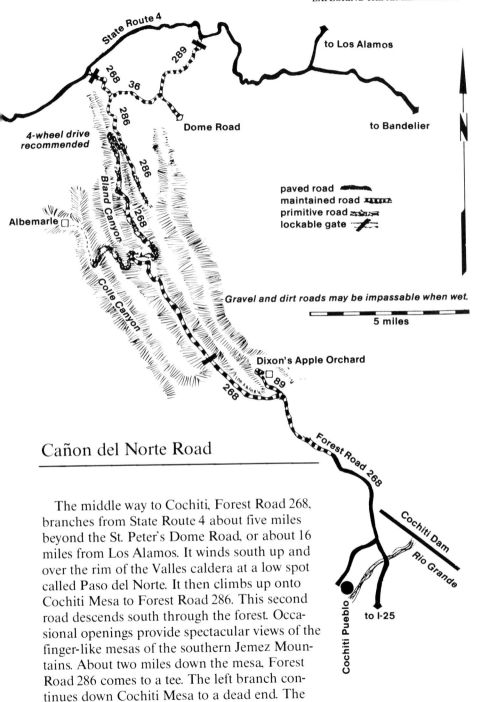

to Los Alamos

State Route 4

289

268

36

286

286

268

Dome Road

to Bandelier

N

4-wheel drive recommended

Bland Canyon

Albemarle

Colle Canyon

paved road
maintained road
primitive road
lockable gate

Gravel and dirt roads may be impassable when wet.

5 miles

Dixon's Apple Orchard

89

268

Cañon del Norte Road

Forest Road 268

Cochiti Dam

Rio Grande

Cochiti Pueblo

to I-25

The middle way to Cochiti, Forest Road 268, branches from State Route 4 about five miles beyond the St. Peter's Dome Road, or about 16 miles from Los Alamos. It winds south up and over the rim of the Valles caldera at a low spot called Paso del Norte. It then climbs up onto Cochiti Mesa to Forest Road 286. This second road descends south through the forest. Occasional openings provide spectacular views of the finger-like mesas of the southern Jemez Mountains. About two miles down the mesa, Forest Road 286 comes to a tee. The left branch continues down Cochiti Mesa to a dead end. The right branch, soon rapidly deteriorating, heads

81

Remains of log cabins are the last traces of homesteaders, miners, herders, and loggers who worked throughout the Jemez country in the late 1800s and early 1900s.

down into Cañon del Norte to rejoin Forest Road 268. Within a few miles Cañon del Norte merges with Medio Dia Canyon—so named because midday is the only time the sun shines in the bottom of this verdant little valley.

As Medio Dia Canyon plunges south, Forest Road 268 continues along the canyon wall out onto lower Horn Mesa, then drops into Bland Canyon. The ghost town of Bland lies in the upper end of the canyon. At the turn of the century it was a profitable, thriving, gold and silver mining community. Named after Richard P. (Silver Dick) Bland of Missouri, it boasted a post office from 1894 to 1935. Now the entrance is barred and the gate is guarded against trespassers. From here one can take a sidetrip to Albemarle.

The Bland Canyon road continues to Cochiti along the south base of Horn Mesa, on whose top rests the prehistoric ruins of Ha-nut Cochiti. The Dixon apple orchard (formerly Old Jim Young's) lies just off this road in Cochiti Canyon.

Trail to Albemarle

Collapsed shacks echo the collapsed dreams of the miners of long ago.

There is a town in the Jemez that people have all but forgotten. Chances are that no one is alive today who once lived there. Only a very few visit this place because it is so difficult to find. The town is Albemarle—next door neighbor and twin sister to Bland. In their day, these two made up the boomingest mining camps in the territory.

Although Bland is still occupied (but fenced in, with a locked gate), time and nature are now the only inhabitants of Albemarle. Every winter snow and every summer rain do their share in returning the remains of man's frenzied endeavors back to the original elements. Gold and silver mining claims were established in this area in 1894. About a dozen mines known as the Albemarle Group were developed by the Cochiti Gold Mining Company, and miners started pouring in from Leadville, Cripple Creek, and Telluride. By 1900, the combined population of Bland and Albemarle was 3,000.

83

A sturdy log cabin
still stands guard on
the road to Albemarle.

In one 4-month period, more than 50 businesses and houses were erected.

Bland was the cultural center, having two banks, a newspaper, hotel, several boarding houses, schools, churches, stores, stock exchange, and opera house, plus saloons, gambling halls, and a red-light district—all squeezed into a canyon only 60 feet wide.

Albemarle, in a still narrower canyon, had most of what Bland boasted, except for the newspaper, stock exchange, and opera house. In addition, Albemarle had several mines on the main street, a 175-ton-per-day stamp mill, a machine shop, a cyanide works for extracting ore, and an electric tramway. The stamp mill was enclosed in the first all-steel structure to be built in New Mexico.

Water for Albemarle was piped from above the falls in Peralta Canyon, over the ridge and down into town. An electrical power line was strung up Colle Canyon from Madrid, 35 miles away. The water supply system and electrical transmission facilities were amazing for those

days in that rough country. Remains of the pipeline can still be found in upper Peralta Canyon, and the old power poles can be seen in Colle Canyon as you hike toward Albemarle.

Four sawmills, employing about 100 men, were turning out lumber day and night in Medio Dia Canyon, but couldn't keep up. Additional lumber had to be hauled in via the Albemarle Stage Line Company, which ran from Albemarle to Thornton, with connections to Albuquerque and Santa Fe.

But just when activities were at their peak, rumors started flying that the ore was running out—and people began leaving. The mine shafts were deepened, but the ore decreased in value. The main ore body occurred in a localized andesite core, surrounded by barren volcanic rock. Mineralization in the core was due to descending, circulating hot water, which created gold- and silver-filled veins in fractures near the ground surface.

In 1902, the stamp mill in Albemarle closed; the post office was discontinued the following

Reminders of days past, like this old leg of a school desk, once littered Albemarle's narrow canyon floor. Souvenir hunters have picked the area clean.

Massive stone foundations attest to the faith of the mining men in the potential wealth of Albemarle.

year. As much equipment as was worth moving was hauled over to Bland, and the town was deserted.

Ghost of an Era

What is Albemarle like today? And how do you get there?

About a quarter mile down Bland Canyon below the locked gate at the entrance to Bland, a dirt road leads off to the west and up the very steep canyon wall. At the top, the road forks, with the left fork going out on West Mesa. The right fork goes down a side gulch into Colle Canyon. This is mining country and some mines are still active. The owners don't like visitors and post their property with NO TRESPASSING signs. But most of the country is U.S. Forest Service land and open to the public.

You can't drive to Albemarle, and sometimes the road is so bad you can't drive into Colle Canyon. It's worth a walk, though; despite all the mining activity, Colle is one of the wildest and most beautiful canyons in the Jemez Mountains. From the canyon floor, a rough

Giant sheave wheels once pulled the hoist at the Albemarle mine. Now, like ghosts of an era, they lie rusted and abandoned.

trail goes up the stream bed. The canyon gets narrower and finally divides. Take the left fork. It is narrower still and could not possibly be wide enough for a wagon road. Keep going up the canyon, for that is the way to Albemarle.

The town is privately owned, but you can walk on Forest Service land to the very edge and see the extent of the activity that took place there so long ago. You'll see rusted remnants of man's presence—bolts, grizzlies (for screening ore), troughs, then a log cabin, and more rusted iron. There are tanks and chutes, stone foundations, mine shafts, huge dilapidated wooden vats, wheels and piping, and a strange lot of convoluted metal shapes whose uses can't be guessed. On the hillsides are scattered piles of weathered boards.

Looking around, you can only marvel at the human energy it took to build this place, and at the hopes and dreams that were realized here—and also shattered. You have the feeling of wanting to touch the remains gently, almost reverently—because they signify the passing of the wild, old-fashioned boom towns. It is not merely the ghost of a town that lies here, it is the ghost of an entire era.

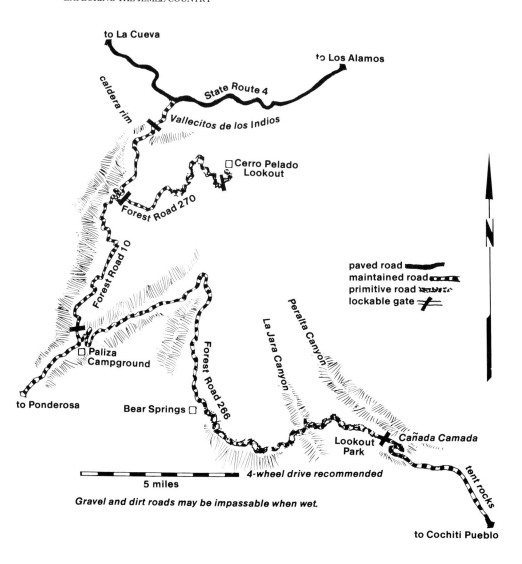

to La Cueva

to Los Alamos

caldera rim

State Route 4

Vallecitos de los Indios

☐ Cerro Pelado
Lookout

Forest Road 270

Forest Road 10

N

paved road
maintained road
primitive road
lockable gate

Peralta Canyon

La Jara Canyon

☐ Paliza
Campground

to Ponderosa

Bear Springs ☐

Forest Road 266

Lookout
Park

Cañada Camada

tent rocks

4-wheel drive recommended

5 miles

Gravel and dirt roads may be impassable when wet.

to Cochiti Pueblo

The Pondersoa Road

The long road to Cochiti is the back road
toward Ponderosa. About 20 miles west of Los
Alamos along State Route 4—past the Valle
Grande, Las Conchas, and the Jemez River
crossings—a sign points off to the left, indicat-
ing that the village of Ponderosa is 16 miles

away. This is Forest Road 10. Forest Road 266 to Cochiti branches off at Paliza Campground about 13 miles over and down the hill.

Dipping down through the pines after leaving State Route 4, Forest Road 10 emerges into a pretty meadow called Vallecitos de los Indios (Spanish for "Little Valleys of the Indians"). Past the meadow, the road climbs rapidly, and from a high, sweeping curve, the dwellings in the *vallecitos* below appear as matchbox-sized buildings. Then the road passes over the rim of the Valles caldera to descend down the southern flank.

Forest Road 10 was built in the early 1900s, then widened and improved in the 1930s by Civilian Conservation Corps crews. The many nicely constructed stone catch basins and culverts beside the road, and along Forest Road 266 to Cochiti, attest to the careful workmanship and cheap labor of those bygone years. Things just aren't made like that anymore.

Redondo Peak, at an elevation of 11,254 feet, is the highest point within the rim of the Valles caldera. Geologically, it is known as a "resurgent dome," a block of magma thrust up by subsequent volcanism long after the caldera had formed.

This cabin down Forest Road 10 to Ponderosa is typical of rustic ranches in the Jemez. It makes you wish the Homestead Act were still in effect, so you could stake a claim to your own mountain meadow.

Room with a View

Nine miles in from the highway, a sign points east up Forest Road 270, a side road to the Cerro Pelado ("Bald Mountain") Fire Lookout. The road to the lookout is narrow but good, winding up through thick stands of young ponderosa pine. Soon the pines change into unending aspen groves, many trees adorned with carvings of names, dates, and backwoods graffiti. The last mile breaks out into open alpine country and the road rapidly becomes 4-wheel drive caliber.

As is traditional with lookouts, the view is superb. If it weren't for the tall trees growing just northeast of the lookout deck, you could see directly down into the Valle Grande. As it is, there are just enough tree tops in the way to make the view into the volcanic caldera merely tantalizing, and not the spectacular scene your imagination says it could be. Just like a country kid in the second row at the big-city parade, you find yourself standing on tiptoe and even jumping up and down to try to gain a few extra inches of height to see over those tree tops.

But the rest of the circle of view makes up for not being able to see the Valle. The Sangre de Cristos, the Sandias, the clear broad sweep of the southern Jemez Mountains and the western Nacimientos stand up big and bold and seemingly just beyond your fingertips. From here, you have a better perspective of the immensity of San Diego and Guadalupe Canyons, and the great stretch of tree-covered mesas and valleys to the south and west.

A Wild Half Acre

Back on Forest Road 10, a little more than halfway to Ponderosa, the road skirts the top edge of a high cliff. From here, a sort of close-in, wide-angle view of lower Paliza Canyon can be seen. Between the road and the cliff edge are a few prize specimens of old, gnarled alligator juniper trees. Although common in other parts of the Southwest, these unique trees with their scale-like bark grow in a narrow range of elevation in the Jemez country. A count of growth rings on a nearby juniper stump indicates about 25 rings to the inch. The largest of the junipers has a diameter of nearly 20 inches, making that tree a true patriarch of the mountains.

Upon descending the cliff, the road passes by what is easily the "wildest half acre" in the Jemez. In a narrow arroyo, the eroded remnants of red-colored volcanic rocks stand up in fantastic shapes. Talk about an eerie, off-world landscape—the likes of these formations are almost beyond description. There are gargoyles, Cleopatra's needles, backs of Triceratops and Stegosaurus dinosaurs, tents, haystacks, exploded solidified bubbles, roller coaster rides—the farthest-out human imagination could not have dreamed up the shapes that exist here.

91

The patterned cracks in its bark give the alligator juniper its name. The author's white hat indicates the size of this giant.

Only a mile or so farther down the canyon, the scenery settles down again to a prosaic and peaceful but pretty canyon as the valley floor levels and widens to provide a location for campsites. The Paliza Campground is here, set amidst big, cinnamon-barked ponderosas. The campground is a fee area; with its many Adirondack-type shelters—built in the 1930s by the Civilian Conservation Corps—it is a good spot for lunch or supper in any kind of weather. From this junction, Forest Road 266 leads east 28 miles across the mountains to Cochiti.

Bear Springs to Tent Rocks

Forest Road 266 deserves a leisurely pace as it cuts through some remarkably pretty mountain country containing green meadows and thick groves of fir and spruce. Watch for catchments along the roadside, additional reminders of the CCC days, when young, single men toiled in the sun for a small wage, much of which was sent home to their families to help tide them over during the Great Depression.

After winding through tribal land of the Jemez Indians and back onto Forest Service turf, the road passes the mothballed Bear Springs Forest Station. The country between here and La Jara Canyon is a prime collecting area for rockhounds. Watch for Apache tears in the roadbed near the forest station. Legend says these small, rounded pieces of black obsidian are the tears shed by Indian maidens in memory of the heroic deeds of their departed loved ones.

Rocks of Ages

The variety of the chalcedony mineral known as Jemez jasper occurs on the hilltop between Bear Springs and La Jara Canyons. Chunks of banded brown jasper can be picked up along the roadside, but the really top-quality specimens are found back in the brush. This part of the Jemez abounds in a myriad variety of chalcedony shapes. The mineral chalcedony is a special form of quartz that has a waxy surface and is usually found as the lining in cavities and the filling in cracks. When chalcedony is colored red or brown by traces of iron, it is called jasper. In the La Jara Canyon area, jasper is found in veins up to 6 inches thick. When the original volcanic rocks began to cool and shrink, silica solutions from deep in the earth filled the cracks with this special form of chalcedony.

The hillsides nearby are covered with slatey slabs of rhyolite, containing reddish bands of

Wind and blowing sand sculpt ledges of red-colored tuff into fanciful shapes, forming magical playgrounds for kids of all ages.

manganese. While not valuable, they are fun to look at because of their astounding symmetrical banding. Also astounding and spectacular is the view. The Rio Grande is a shining ribbon winding south between wide bands of cottonwood bosque. Its broad valley is guarded on the east by the jagged wall of Ortiz and San Pedro Mountains. The rounded mass of Sandia Mountain looms like a giant watermelon to the southeast. Off to the southwest, Ladrone ("Thief") Mountain lurks like a mysterious sentinel, while massive Mount Taylor, named for President Zachary Taylor, dominates the western horizon.

The road dips quickly through La Jara Canyon, then skirts the foothills across piñon-covered mesas. Before the road drops off the plateau, the high vantage point of Lookout Park provides a view into the bottom of Peralta Canyon. Here, Peralta is joined by a side canyon with the poetic name of Cañada Camada. For a short distance, the combined canyons have a broad flat bottom with their walls rising 700 feet to the rim. This huge amphitheater of red and

white cliffs is inspiring in all kinds of lighting. Tent rocks line the bottom and march part way up the steep lower slopes. It's like having Bryce Canyon mixed in a circular bowl with Canyon de Chelly. The name *camada* means "litter," "brood," or "nest." Any one of these names could apply as this amphitheater looks like a big nest filled with a litter of tent rocks.

Soon Forest Road 266 contorts into a few hairpin turns and drops suddenly into Peralta Canyon. On the broad canyon floor, the road passes by another impressive stand of tent rocks, but of quite a different variety. These tents aren't the usual kind found around the northern part of the Jemez. They are formed of many layers of stratified pumice beds, laid down in the quiet water of a prehistoric lake. Mingled with the pumice particles are small pieces of black obsidian, rounded by erosion. These pea-sized bits of volcanic glass are more Apache tears.

Although of identical chemical composition, obsidian and pumice are formed in different

The tent rocks in lower Peralta Canyon are composed of stratified pumice layers and contain small bits of rounded obsidian known as "Apache tears."

95

ways. Obsidian is essentially a hardened liquid:
molten rock that cooled too fast for crystals to
form. Pumice, at the other extreme, is the same
kind of molten rock, but was mixed with gas or
air and became frothy before it cooled, perhaps
by being thrown high into the atmosphere.
These two opposite types came together through
the processes of erosion and deposition. They
were eroded from their place of origin, carried
away by ancient flood waters, and deposited
briefly into these wondrous shapes before being
swept away again in nature's ceaseless
rearrangements.

Drums Along the Rio

The final noteworthy items of the trip to
Cochiti are the water tanks at the pueblo.
Usually water tanks aren't especially appealing,
but these are worth a second look and maybe
even a picture. They reflect both the Indian's
humor and his eye for potential beauty in all
objects. The tanks are painted to resemble tribal
drums. The Cochiti are renowned throughout
the Rio Grande country for their drum-making
skills, and their tanks serve as unique advertise-
ments of their specialty.

Year of the Nut

"Hey, look! Instant landscaping," was Mary's first exclamation on seeing the piñon forests of New Mexico.

Our initial glimpse of the little trees came in a bright September. We were immediately captivated by their shape and their scent, and by the unending stretch of them over the changing landscape. In the canyon country around Los Alamos and on the rolling hills near Santa Fe, the piñon tree rarely grows higher than 15 to 20 feet. To call such a collection of diminutive trees a forest may not be entirely correct, but no other term seems quite appropriate either. There are thousands upon thousands of acres of them, each one a perfect specimen of unique individuality, all looking like oversized Japanese bonsai trees.

It seemed incredible that we could have lived so long without knowing that such an enchanting life form existed. When we became better acquainted with them, there was an even bigger treat in store—the piñon nut.

September and October are always the best months in the Southwest. It's as if the piñon tree knows this and wants to contribute its all for man's increased pleasure. The pitch seems to exude its own additional special odor, giving a bracing tang to the already sparkling autumn air. At this time of year, the green piñon cones suddenly turn brown, opening almost inside out in their eagerness to give their fruit to the world.

Someone once said that the taste of the piñon nut is like pine and sunshine and popcorn, and peanuts too in a way. The meat is so delightfully delicious, and yet so devilishly hard to extract from the shell.

Old-time New Mexicans have a way of cracking the shells with their teeth that makes it easy—if you can master the process. The nuts go in one side of the mouth and the empty

Branches, cones, and nuts of the piñon. Note in the cone the large cavities that cradle mature nuts. Photo by John V. Young.

shells come out the other. Try putting two or three nuts in your mouth to start with. Stand a nut upright between the back molars and apply pressure until the shell cracks lengthwise. Separate the two halves of the shell with your tongue and flick the kernel out. Move the empty shell to the other side of your mouth, spit it out, and chew up the kernel, then proceed to attack the next nut. Soon you'll be able to work your way through half a dozen nuts at a time.

Politics and piñon nuts have a special affinity in New Mexico. At fall political rallies, the speakers have grown used to the cracking and munching of their audiences. The floors of meeting halls are often covered with empty shells when the people finally get up to go. Schoolroom floors and desks are also favorite gathering places for piñon shells.

All neophyte piñoneros should take note that World Series telecasts and college football games provide great times to practice no-hands piñon nut eating.

The picking of *piñones* is an art in itself and is as varied as the individual picker. The main idea is to get the nuts off the tree and into the container in the easiest way possible. Some people shake the tree; others beat the branches with brooms to dislodge the nuts. Laying blankets or tarps under the tree to catch the falling nuts has become a favorite method of collecting. Others like to get closer to their work and pick the nuts off the ground with their fingers. By picking them up individually, you can be selective and gather only the good ones—maybe.

Not all of the nuts that come down from the tree are filled—some are empty shells that have never matured. When you gather *piñones*, pick up only the dark brown nuts that have a slightly oily sheen. All the rest are usually empty. There is nothing more discouraging than to arrive home and find that only half your nuts are good. When you get the nuts home, dump your pickings into a pan of water; the filled shells will sink to the bottom or stay just below the surface. The empties will float high, more than half out of the water. If you doubt that they are really empty, try cracking open a few.

Now for the roasting. Spread them on a tray in a 350-degree Fahrenheit oven for half an hour or so. Keep tasting them to make sure they are not over-roasted. Usually they are done when the meat takes on a yellowish tinge.

A good crop of *piñones* comes along every five to seven years, depending on what you like to believe. Actually, it takes two years for the cones and nuts to mature. If the conditions of moisture and fertilization are right, good crops can theoretically occur every other year, but they rarely do. The easiest way for a neophyte to recognize a good year is to watch the roadsides in piñon country, starting in September. Cars line the roadsides and numerous pickers kneel under the trees filling their bags and boxes.

New Mexico natives have long considered the piñon nut to be a true gift of God, available to everyone for the picking. Fortunately the U.S. Forest Service in New Mexico shares similar views, believing the nuts belong to the people. Consequently, no permits are issued to commercial pickers. *Piñones* are a commercial crop. In some years they bring over 50 million dollars to the southwestern states.

Keep an eye out for a Year of the Nut.

BANDELIER BACK PACK

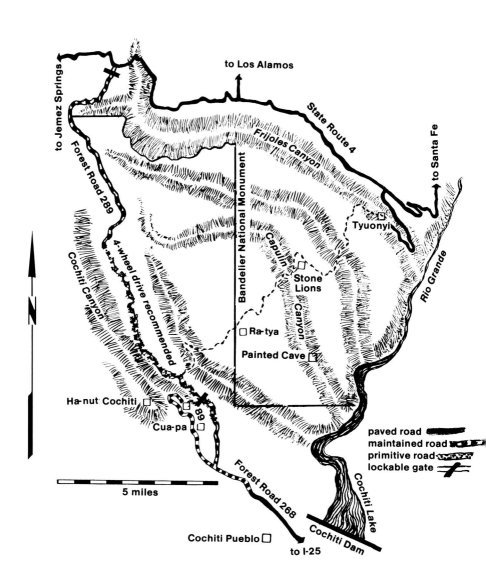

Gravel and dirt roads may be impassable when wet.

Bandelier Back Pack

"If you want to feel the power and pathos of time, roll up in your blankets some night on any one of a hundred mesas, or in any one of a hundred canyons of the old abandoned land of the Pajaritans. The stars that sparkle down on you watched over the cataclysm that rent the nearby mountains, ... saw the mesas rise out of the chaos, the rifts deepen into gorges; ... saw cliffs and caves shaped by wind and rain; and, at last, saw human life drift quietly in, take up the routine of orderly existence, then quietly flow on into the ocean which we call Time. Listen to the winds that sang through the pines a thousand years ago—melodies that, unknown and unnoticed through silent centuries, have never ceased and never will."

Edgar L. Hewett wrote those words for the preface of his book, *The Pajarito Plateau and Its Ancient People*, published in 1938 by the School of American Research.

The Wandering Cochitis

The legends of the Cochiti Indians indicate that their ancestors made an incredible series of moves across the mesas and canyons of the Pajarito Plateau before settling on the Rio Grande. Sometime after 1350 A.D., a group of 400 to 500 people left the circular pueblo of Tyuonyi in Frijoles Canyon and moved five miles south to create the city now known as the Pueblo of the Stone Lions. After an undetermined time and cause, the tribe moved down into Capulin Canyon near Painted Cave. Then again they moved, up to the mesa top on the west to build Ra-tya, or San Miguel Pueblo. From there, they moved to Cua-pa in Cochiti Canyon, and then to the top of precipitous Horn Mesa to build Ha-nut Cochiti ("Cochiti

101

Above"). By the time Coronado arrived, they had moved down to the present Cochiti Pueblo.

A friend from Los Alamos, Jim Reavis, and I had often talked of back-packing across the back country of Bandelier National Monument, following the trail of the Cochiti. We wanted to spend a night at each one of those abandoned prehistoric pueblos, to poke about the ruins and try to get a feeling for the personality of the place, to experience what Hewett wrote about.

To simplify transportation, Jim and I decided to follow the Cochiti travels in reverse, starting at the pueblo of Ha-nut and hiking back toward the original settlement in Frijoles Canyon. We did it during the last week of October—when the moon was full, flocks of Canada geese were overhead, and the last wildflowers were still in bloom.

The total distance covered was only about 30 miles, which left plenty of time each day for exploring, as well as for hiking on to the next ruins. During our five days in the back country, we didn't see another human. We came away from the experience agreeing that those days of solitude seemed to heighten the mood that Hewett was able to capture in his writings of the Pajarito Plateau.

Ha-nut Cochiti

Built as a square-shaped stronghold city, the pueblo of Ha-nut Cochiti lies near the end of the narrow fingertip of Horn Mesa between Cochiti and Bland Canyons. It can be reached by a strenuous climb up the steep slope behind the Dixon apple ranch (formerly Old Jim Young's orchards) off Forest Road 268. The entire Cañada de Cochiti Grant is now the property of the University of New Mexico, having been deeded to the school by Jim Young. Permission to enter the ruins can be obtained at the ranch.

Although Ha-nut was abandoned before Coronado came up the Rio Grande, it was reoccupied during the Pueblo Revolt of 1680-92. When Spanish rule was absent, several groups of Indians moved back up to the old pueblo for protection against the lawlessness of their brothers. Upon the Spaniards' return, the Indians on Horn Mesa constituted one of the last pockets of resistance to the reconquest. In the spring of 1694, Diego de Vargas stormed the fortress with 150 soldiers, killing 21 of the defenders before the final surrender.

As Ha-nut was one of the rare prehistoric pueblos to be occupied again in historic time, the walls of the ruins still have adobe plaster clinging to them. Prints of the hands that smoothed the adobe walls can still be seen.

From the top of Horn Mesa, site of Ha-nut Cochiti, the apple orchards of the Dixon Ranch in Cochiti Canyon provide some interesting geometric designs.

Cua-pa

The ruins of Cua-pa lie along Forest Road 268 two miles down the valley to the east of Ha-nut. This was a huge pueblo, built entirely of large, rounded river stones, instead of the usual volcanic tuff blocks. The interior plaza of Cua-pa was over 100 yards across, big enough to play several games of football at once. The total pueblo was nearly one-half mile long and contained many multistoried dwellings. Mounds of cholla-covered rubble are all that is left of this once-great complex; however, on the extreme eastern edge, there are some walls still standing, which may be evidence of occupation during the revolt.

About a mile and a half farther downstream from Cua-pa, where Bland Creek flows into Rio Chiquito, there are several prehistoric rock shelters at the base of the basalt cliffs. Here, on the roofs and walls of the shelters, is an amazing array of pictographs that are some of the best in the Southwest. They are worthy of preservation, but they'll probably be destroyed in a few years, as they are literally across the street from the nearby Cochiti City development.

Ra-tya

From the pumice mine in Eagle Canyon off Forest Road 289, a rough trail leads north into Bandelier National Monument. Nestled in the wild mesas east of the trail was the third home of the Cochiti.

The pueblo of Ra-tya, also called San Miguel, was built on a high mesa close to the wooded slopes of the Jemez Mountains. The pueblo once consisted of five separate multistoried buildings arranged around a small central plaza. Two kivas were within the plaza and an artificial reservoir was outside. Hewn blocks of volcanic tuff rock, some as long as 40 inches and usually chinked with smaller pieces, were used in the construction of the pueblo walls. This ruin, as well as most of the other large complexes, was partially excavated by Hewett in the early 1900s.

Painted Cave

These figures enlivening the wall of Painted Cave in the Bandelier Wilderness look like they belong in a prehistoric comic strip. The creatures with the white gloves are about to have their tails snapped off by a hungry coyote.

There is somewhat of a mystery concerning the ruins near Painted Cave in Capulin Canyon. Not enough ruins are present to have housed all the people who supposedly lived there. A few cave dwellings and talus houses were located near the cave, and several small pueblos, which contained 10 to 20 rooms each, were constructed on the valley floor. But nowhere in the vicinity are to be found ruins that compare in size with the rest of the legendary homes of the Cochiti.

Painted Cave itself still remains as remarkable as ever, a glorious picture gallery in a shallow arch. Most impressive are a full-scale drawing of an elk and a larger-than-life profile of a monkey. Evidently, a traveling tribe from Central America had a monkey as a mascot and the dwellers at Painted Cave were inspired to paint his picture. A short distance down-canyon from the big cave is a smaller one, its interior painted entirely in red, with dozens of crosses of all sizes incised into the rock surfaces.

Stone Lions

The Pueblo of the Stone Lions contained more than 300 rooms on the ground floor and was possibly four stories high. There were four kivas within the interior plaza and two outside—one nearly as big as the largest kiva at Tyuonyi. East of the pueblo, the inhabitants scooped a water reservoir out of the soft tuff rock. Nearby was the Shrine of the Stone Lions, the most important hunting shrine in the entire Pueblo region. Two carved figures of crouching mountain lions, tails extended, heads pointing east, still lie within an enclosure of upended stone slabs.

After the glorious purple flowers of autumn fade, shining white aster heads herald the coming of winter.

And Other Unforgettable Memories

... while camped at San Miguel, seeing a blood-red moon rising over the Sangre de Cristos.

... a set of magnificent petroglyphs, stretching for 200 feet along the cliff face, in a remote canyon on the Cañada-Capulin Trail.

... a continuous concert of birdsong. I now know where the birds go in October: they are all in the back country at Bandelier—finches, robins, juncos, chickadees, sparrows, grosbeaks, bluebirds, flycatchers, flickers, and woodpeckers.

As we hiked along, I got to wondering how many seconds would elapse between the songs of the birds that we heard. When one song ended, I started to count—and never got past the count of "one" before I heard another bird start to sing. All day long, for three days.

The Garden on the Frijoles

Taking the trek in reverse proved to be an effective way to compare all the ruins. After seeing the other sites, we had a deeper appreciation

In autumn, the curled seed-heads of blue grama resemble tiny sickles. This grass is a dominant plant of the piñon-juniper mesas.

for the peace and beauty of Frijoles Canyon. Hiking down the long, sloping trail on the south side of the canyon toward Bandelier National Monument headquarters, we caught the whole panorama of the ancient civilization spread out below. From Ceremonial Cave, past the Long House talus village to Tyuonyi and Rainbow House, this lovely valley must have been like the Garden of Eden to the Cochiti. They never again lived in such an idyllic spot after they left this Garden on the Rito de los Frijoles.

AND STILL SO MUCH MORE

In July and August, early morning fog in the Valle Grande gives the surrounding forest a "Day of Creation" look.

The list of things to see and do in the Jemez goes on and on. You can drive to Camp May above Los Alamos in early October to see the golden aspen. You can drive along the Rio Guadalupe through the old railway tunnels in Guadalupe Box on the way to the ghost lumber towns farther up the canyon. You can visit San Ildefonso, Santa Clara, and Jemez Pueblos on

their feast days. You can go on a Night Walk
led by a ranger in Bandelier.

In the summer, Santa Clara Canyon is always
one of the loveliest spots in the mountains, in
spite of the great numbers of campers that go
there.

In the winter, devotees of Christmas lighting
take delight in the displays at Jemez Springs
during the holiday season. American Indian
nativity and shepherd scenes give a local flavor
to the familiar story. And for that old-fashioned
Christmas feeling, visit the Catholic churches in
the villages of Abiquiu, Cañones, and Capulin.

There is one particular Bible verse that
always seems appropriate wherever I go in the
Jemez.

Una cosa he demandado del Señor, . . .

para contemplar la hermosura del Señor.

One thing have I asked of the Lord, . . .

to behold the beauty of the Lord.
— Psalms 27:4

Roland Pettitt (1924 - 1987) scientist, author, humanitarian.

ROLAND A. PETTITT
1924 - 1987

Roland Pettitt's first book was published in 1972. Entitled *Los Alamos—Before the Dawn*, it described the early history of the Jemez Mountains, before the scientists arrived at the dawn of the atomic age. This, his second book, *Exploring the Jemez Country*, was first published in 1975.

The author was raised in the Yakima Valley of Washington State. He attended Washington State University, receiving degrees in both geology and civil engineering. Over a 10-year period, the Pettitt family—Roland, his wife Mary, and children Jean, Susan, and Jeff—moved around the country as Roland worked on various hydroelectric and water-supply projects. The move to Los Alamos came in 1961. He and Mary soon regarded New Mexico as their home. Their love affair with the Jemez country never diminished.

Until his final illness, Roland was employed by Los Alamos National Laboratory on geothermal research projects, then in engineering liaison. He was author of numerous technical and professional papers and wrote feature articles for the *Los Alamos Monitor* as well as other area newspapers.

The Pettitts worked tirelessly for the betterment of the Los Alamos community. Roland was especially interested in young people and was active in Boy Scouts and his local church. He and Mary participated in civic beautification efforts. They were also active beyond Los Alamos County, supporting homes for young people such as Jemez House and New Mexico Girls and Boys Ranches. One of Roland's last projects was an effort to promote world peace and understanding.

DOROTHY HOARD

Dorothy Hoard has been Roland Pettitt's alter ego in preparing for publication this Second Edition of *Exploring the Jemez Country.* A resident of Los Alamos since 1963, she shares Roland's enthusiasm for the Jemez Mountains and has spent countless hours alone and with family and friends hiking and driving in the area.

Dorothy grew up in Salinas, California, and earned a degree in biochemistry from the University of California at Berkeley. Her family includes husband Donald and four grown children. Since 1974, she has been employed as a chemical technician at the Los Alamos National Laboratory. She is also an accomplished artist, in both watercolor painting and pen-and-ink illustration, and has devised the ingenious three-dimensional style maps which introduce sections of this book.

As an avid observer and interpreter of the outdoors, Dorothy has written and illustrated two books: *A Guide to Bandelier National Monument* and *Los Alamos Outdoors.* She also illustrated and co-authored, with Teralene Foxx, *Flowers of the Southwestern Forests and Woodlands.*

In 1986, she received a governor's award for investigating the archaeology and rock art of the Pajarito Plateau and a national citation for her efforts to establish the Bandelier and Dome Wildernesses. Since then, she has continued documenting the petroglyphs of the area and has founded the volunteer Friends of Bandelier to support her favorite park.